MONETARISM

MONETARISM

How the Financial Crisis Can Help You
Make Money in the Stock Market

THOMAS R. IRELAND

ARLINGTON HOUSE
NEW ROCHELLE, N. Y.

Library of Congress Catalog Card Number 73-18186

Manufactured in the United States of America

Library of Congress Cataloging in Publication Data

Ireland, Thomas R
  Monetarism; how the financial crisis can help you
make money in the stock market.

    1. Money--United States. 2. Monetary policy--
United States. 3. Investments--United States.
I. Title.
HG538.I7   332.4'6   73-18186
ISBN 0-87000-235-X

To my grandfathers,
who taught me more
than I could ever repay,
OTHO T. IRELAND AND HARRY E. PRATT

Contents

Introduction

When Richard Nixon took office as President of the United States in January 1969, it was widely heard that the economic philosophy of "monetarism" would supplant the Keynesian doctrine as the dominant economic policy orientation of the federal government. Milton Friedman, the godfather of monetarism, was rumored to be among Nixon's closest advisors on monetary matters and economics in general. Even from Nixon himself came indications that he would rely on monetary policy to stem the tide of the inflation which still plagues this nation.

In the first two months of the Nixon administration, evidence became even stronger. William McChesney Martin, then chairman of the powerful Federal Reserve Board, resigned. Many observers speculated that Martin had resigned with the private understanding that Nixon would appoint as his replacement Arthur F. Burns. Burns was a long-time friend of Nixon and one of Milton Friedman's teachers at Rutgers University. Burns was also a man whose recent statements had indicated that he was moving in the direction of a monetarist position. So it was said. Martin did resign. Burns was appointed. The so-called reign of monetarism was to begin.*

---

* See *Time*, 19 December, pp. 66-72, and Milton Viorst, "Friedmanism, n., Doctrine of Most Audacious U.S. Economist; esp. Theory 'Only Money Matters,'" *New York Times Magazine*, 25 January 1970, pp. 22-23, 80-84.

Under Burns's direction, the Federal Reserve Board busied itself with causing the present recession. Burns and his colleagues did follow a policy which would have produced a reduction in inflation in the long run. It would also have caused a depression if it had been continued long enough. From May 1969 to February 1970 the Federal Reserve Board caused the total amount of money outstanding in the United States to remain almost constant. The seeds of the recession were sown. Nineteen seventy was the beginning of one of the longest lingering recessions in recent history.

Fortunately, the Federal Reserve Board reversed its policy in March 1970 and began behaving erratically instead of perversely. Much more dire consequences were thereby averted. It was in this period that Nixon and Burns parted company and Nixon began mumbling that he had become a "Keynesian." With a return to its old policies, the Federal Reserve Board rekindled the inflationary fires which had barely subsided. During this period, the nation got very little inflation abatement for its recessionary misery. The celebrated reign of monetarism had ended.

Or so it was said. Nothing which had happened during this period was contrary to the theory of monetarism. Monetarists, indeed, were first among the nation's economists to predict the 1970 recession. It was not monetarism, but monetary policy, that enjoyed favor with the early Nixon administration. Monetarism is, to be sure, a philosophy of economic relationships that stresses the importance of the money supply in determining economic events. It does not, however, suggest that *any* policy based on the importance of money is desirable.

To blame monetarism for the 1970-72 recession is the height of irony. What was done before and during that period was the most perfect antimonetarist monetary policy since the Great Depression. During most of the history of the Federal Reserve System (1914 to the present), the Federal Reserve Board has not paid much attention to the money supply. Most of the recessions and the Great Depression itself were accidents caused by Federal Reserve interest in other matters. But for the 1970 recession, the Federal Reserve Board, under Burns, continued deliberately to follow a policy of contracting the money supply so severely that a recession became inevitable.

The recession came. Monetarism was blamed. President Nixon turned to "Keynesianism" in word, and reliance on wage and price controls in practice. That monetarism had had its chance and failed was heard among "experts" who had never understood the theory of monetarism or what it implied on a policy level.

Monetarism was *not* tried by the Nixon administration. It was *not* tried by the Federal Reserve Board under Arthur Burns. And it has *not* failed. Monetarism is an economic philosophy whose theory and policy has not commanded the allegiance of political leaders and whose promise will not be realized until it is understood by the public far better than it is today.

Monetarism has not had a favorable press. Before Milton Friedman, it had almost no press at all. It is not understood by the public or the media. The fault for this lack of understanding, however, does not lie with the media or the public. Rather, it lies with the economists who wear its mantle. There has been little real concern among monetarist economists to communicate their ideas and intellectual defense to the public at large.

This book attempts to dispel some of the misunderstanding which surrounds monetarism. In the process, it may give the reader some basis on which to judge his own alternatives as they depend on economic conditions of the future.

Chapter One

Basic Ideas
of Economics

The heart of economics is the interaction of the basic forces of supply and demand. Each individual and firm—and even governments—react to signals generated by the forces of supply and demand. As individuals and firms react, the economy as a whole reacts, however small the change. Supply and demand determine prices, but prices are the basis on which individuals change supply and demand. It is an open-ended process, but one whose logic can put in order basic economic reasoning.

Some economists are fond of pointing out the "fallacy of composition" in mundane reasoning about economic problems— that it is a fallacy to assume that what is true for the individual or firm is true for the economy as a whole. That may be, but the difference between an individual and a total economy is not as

13

absolute as it is sometimes made out to be. Nothing changes in an economy that does not derive from or relate to changes in the behavior of individuals, reacting on an individual basis to economic signals generated by supply and demand. The whole, in some important respects, may have different characteristics than its parts, but the whole cannot be understood without understanding its parts—a fact ignored by some highly sophisticated, but grievously wrong economists.

Thus, to begin, it is necessary to look at fundamental units and fundamental forces. The fundamental units in the American economy are individuals, firms and governments. Individuals act as consumers and demanders of goods and services and as ultimate owners and suppliers of resources. Firms act as producers and suppliers of goods and services and as purchasers and demanders of the services of resources owned by individuals. (When corporations own plant and other types of physical capital equipment, these resources are ultimately owned by the stockholders who are, of course, individuals.) Governments act partly in a manner similar to firms in buying resources, but with the crucial difference that their decisions are guided partly in terms of national policy (or at least political policy). Governments will be discussed later, but here it will be useful to look in more detail at individuals and firms.

The Individual

In a modern economy, individual economic decisions can be broken down into four basic categories, each one of which has implications for the total economy. First, individuals must decide how much of their time to rent to employers or use for labor if self-employed and how much to enjoy as leisure. For the economy as a whole, the decisions of all workers with respect to this question will partially determine the potential labor supply and thereby partially determine the total amount of goods and services that will be produced. Larger offerings of labor services from a given population can be used to produce more goods and services, provided that they are properly utilized.

Second, individuals must decide how much of their incomes to save and how much to use for current consumption. As individuals consume, they use income to claim goods and services that will soon be used up or, in effect, destroyed. As they save, they make goods and services they could have claimed available for the productive purposes of investment rather than the destructive purposes of consumption.

In some types of economic theory, saving is treated as a negative factor in the economic process which must be compensated for by private investment or government spending. Nothing could be more misleading. Saving by individuals provides the wherewithal for progress. Amounts saved may not immediately be converted into investment goods, but only saving can create financial capital necessary for the production of investment goods.

Third, within the portions of an individual's income he decides to consume, he must decide what to consume—how much of this and how much of that. For the economy as a whole, the decisions of individuals in this respect will partially determine how much of each different good or service will be produced and what their prices will be. As individuals in general want more oranges and fewer apples, the price and production level of oranges will tend to rise and the price and production level of apples will tend to fall.

Fourth, as individuals save, they must determine the form of saving. In investment theory, this is called portfolio determination. As individuals decide to save parts of their incomes, they must hold saved income in the form of assets. Assets may be broken down into "real" and "financial" categories. Real assets are equities that involve the actual ownership of resources, including a person's ownership of his own person as a labor source. A real asset must involve something tangible although it need not be easily accessible to the individual. A common stock in a corporation is a real asset because it is a fractional ownership of the

15

physical holdings of a corporation. Real estate, or individually owned tractors or trucks, are easier examples.

Financial assets are assets that involve the ownership of or a claim on money. Financial assets include monies, near monies and bonds. What monies are is a matter of controversy among economists. Milton Friedman argues that monies include currency, demand deposits (checking account balances), and time deposits (savings account balances in commercial banks). This is called the M_2 definition. The M_1 definition accepted by most nonmonetarist economists includes currency and demand deposits only. Near monies include such things as cash surrender value of whole life insurance policies, savings accounts in savings and loans or mutual savings banks and savings certificates. Near monies are really financial assets which are somewhat like money and somewhat like bonds, but technically not either. Bonds are any type of promises to pay fixed amounts of money in the future. This would include short term notes and paper, bills, promises, auto loans and so forth.

From the standpoint of the economy as a whole, the particular types of assets individuals choose will have effects on interest rates and will determine the ease with which saved income can be converted to real productive assets. More on this later.

The Firm

In the American economy, the firm exists to organize the productive process. The primary objective of firm behavior is to generate profits, which are then either used to finance further expansion of the firm or paid out as dividends to stockholders.

Firms obtain resources in three basic ways. They may buy resources in three basic ways. They may buy resources directly out of earnings or by sale of new stock. When this happens, these resources become part of the underlying "realness" of the real assets owned by stockholders in the form of shares in the firm. The firm may borrow in order to buy resources. In this case, the acquisition of new resources is matched by bonded indebtedness. To do this, the firm must issue bonds or a note equal in value to the acquired assets. The firm may also rent its resources rather than owning them outright. It must necessarily rent its labor resources because slavery is illegal. (A one-man enterprise can technically be said to own its own human resources, but this is really a matter of twisting language.)

What a firm does with resources is to arrange them in such a way as to minimize costs of production. In doing this, it finds the combinations of resources that can most efficiently produce any given amount of a product. That includes the size of the firm itself. To the degree that it succeeds more than other firms, it earns higher profits for its owners.

The Role of Prices

Decisions of both individuals and firms depend on prices. Prices determine the ratios at which one thing can be traded for another. In turn, prices are determined by the supply and demand for each item in question. The individual decision with respect to the portion of his time he will use in providing labor services will depend at least partially on the price, or wage rate, he is paid for each hour of labor he provides. As he decides how much he will consume and how much he will save, his decision will be influenced by the price, or interest rate, he will be paid for saving or must pay for borrowing. As he decides which consumer goods and services to buy and which assets to buy, he will take into account the ratios between the prices of various goods and assets. These ratios will tell him how much of one thing he must give up to get a certain amount of another.

Likewise, as firms try to combine resources into the cheapest possible production techniques, they will take into account the prices of each type of resource they could use. The combination actually selected depends both on resource productivity and on resource prices.

Prices, however, are affected as individuals and firms make

17

these decisions. In this respect, today's prices affect tomorrow's economic decisions even though today's prices reflect yesterday's economic decisions. It is at this point that the fallacy of composition problem enters the picture. To an individual or a small firm, a price is a constant—a fact about the world in which he or it exists. On the basis of this fact, individuals and firms make economic decisions. The decisions of no one individual or firm (a very large firm creates an exception) will have any effect on a price that is noticeable to the individual or firm.

Individuals and firms in everyday practice are constantly making changes in their behavior, but in a stable situation, changes in one direction tend to cancel changes in the opposite direction. That is what creates a "stable" situation. In a stable situation, prices do not change. But when many individuals or firms decide to change their behavior in a given direction (and it is much more likely that it would be individuals who decide to do so first), other forces are set in motion and an unstable situation develops. The unstable situation will lead to changes in prices, which in turn will lead to further changes in individual and firm behavior, setting off an ever widening set of interacting price and behavior changes that becomes smaller and smaller until a new stable situation emerges. How and why this happens is the matter of supply and demand.

Supply and Demand

To individuals of even the remotest degree of economic sophistication, the notion that supply and demand determine prices is hardly new. Still, there are special aspects of how this happens that are extremely important in explaining how and why recessions and inflations come about. For that reason, it will be worthwhile to review the process.

Potential buyers, or demanders, of any good, service or asset value the item they are willing to buy in terms of a number of considerations unique to themselves. Vegetarians don't, in general, buy guns to go hunting. Nor do football players buy mini-

18

skirts. Among the factors that determine how much a person wants of a given item are two factors central to economic theory. One is the price of the good and the other is the income of the individual. Demand schedules, as shown in Table 1, are based on the assumption that dollar incomes and all other noneconomic factors are held at a constant level. This is done to isolate the impact of prices on the quantities of the item the individual (or firm) wants. Table 1 presents a hypothetical demand schedule for bunches of carrots.

Table 1

Hypothetical Demand Schedule

$/bunch	Carrots demanded (in 000s of bunches)
$1.00	750
.90	1400
.80	2000
.70	2700
.60	3500
.50	4400
.40	5000
.30	5500
.20	5900
.10	6200

The effect of price on quantity demanded is that of determining how much money must be given up to acquire bunches of carrots. As prices fall, individuals will be willing to purchase more. At higher prices they will purchase less.

Potential sellers, or suppliers, of any good, service or asset determine the amounts they are willing to sell in terms of the prices they can receive for producing *or giving up* items for sale. Supply schedules, as shown in Table 2, are based on the assumption that all factors except the price of the item in question are held constant.

Table 2

Hypothetical Supply Schedule

$/bunch	Carrots supplied (in 000s of bunches)
$1.00	10,000
.90	9,000
.80	8,000
.70	7,000
.60	6,000
.50	5,500
.40	5,000
.30	4,500
.20	4,000
.10	3,500

Table 2 presents a hypothetical supply schedule for carrots. Under these circumstances, the only stable price would be 40¢ per bunch because at that price suppliers wish to sell 5 million bunches and demanders wish to buy 5 million bunches. Everyone will be able to realize his plans for responding to a price of 40¢ per bunch. If, however, the price were at 60¢ per bunch, suppliers would attempt to sell 6 million bunches whereas buyers would be willing to buy only 3½ million (figures from Tables 1 and 2).

In the standard way of looking at things, this would mean a surplus of carrots on the market and suppliers would begin to reduce prices in order to eliminate the surplus. As they did so, future carrot supplies would be reduced because of lower returns on carrot production. Demanders would become willing to buy larger amounts of carrots as prices fell, the process of price reduction coupled with increased carrot purchases continuing until all carrots just cleared the market at the stable price of 40¢.

If the price had been 30¢ to start with, demanders trying to buy 5½ million bunches would have bid up the price to 40¢, thereby reducing their own desired purchases to 5 million while the higher price induced suppliers to increase the amounts they supplied to that level.

A Deeper Look

So much for the standard way of looking at things. It isn't wrong, but it isn't the whole picture either—and the rest of the picture is extremely important for theories trying to explain the behavior of the total economy. Suppose that 30¢ was a previous stable price for carrots. This would have been before the economy had moved to the demand schedule in Table 1. At 30¢, the same stable situation we now find at 40¢ would have existed, although with a smaller amount of carrots produced. Now, for some reason, individuals increase their desires for carrots and the entire demand schedule shifts to that indicated in Table 1. As this occurs, the shortage of 2 million bunches (demanders want 5½ million and suppliers are willing to supply only 4½ million) discussed earlier comes into existence. At this point, the adjustment process begins to carry the price and level of production to higher levels in the manner described earlier.

But the ignored question is: *Why* did the demand for carrots increase and what are the implications of that reason for the rest of the economy? There is a number of possible answers, each type of which has different implications. The answers will provide a first "feel" for what an economic process really means.

If individuals become willing to buy more carrots at each possible price than previously, this willingness must be matched by a willingness to give up something else in order to acquire more carrots. Demand is measured in terms of willingness to pay the price asked. Willingness to pay implies a willingness to give something up—either money itself or something that money could be used to buy. If individuals have become willing to buy more carrots than previously at a price of 30¢ per bunch, they must also have become willing to give up something of equal value in order to acquire the additional carrots.

By a small amount of mathematical reasoning, it is obvious that before individuals increased their demands for carrots, they were willing to pay $1,350,000 for 4½ million bunches of carrots. After the demand increase, the dollar amount increases

21

to $1,650,000 for a net increase of $300,000. Even though, because of supply factors, they cannot actually buy this amount, their willingness to do so implies that they would be willing to give up $300,000 worth of something else to acquire more carrots.

Whatever they are willing to give up, they have, in effect, reduced their demands for. They could give up parsnips, or money or stocks or bonds, but they must give up something. That something will probably be some combination of different things, but regardless, demands for these things will have fallen and by an amount equal to $300,000. Because an increased willingness to buy carrots implies a willingness not to buy or keep something else, the increased demand for carrots must be matched by a reduced set of demands somewhere else. Those reduced demands will cause surpluses just as the increased demand for carrots will cause a shortage. And, as the price of carrots begins to rise, those prices will begin to fall.

Price Level Effects

Carrots are not terribly important in the context of the American economy, but even so, if the price of carrots goes up and no other price goes down, the average of prices will have risen slightly —very slightly perhaps, but crucially nevertheless for an understanding of total economic adjustments.

Averages of various kinds of prices are called price indexes, of which some of the most common are the cost of living index, the retail price index, the wholesale price index and the general price level. All of these indexes, however, take into account only the prices of newly produced goods and services. None of them take into account prices of assets, including money itself, except for those real assets which are currently being produced as capital goods and are therefore both goods and assets at the same time.

This is important because in this fact lies the determination of whether or not an increase in the price of any one good, in this case carrots, will have inflationary effects. If the things individuals give up to buy carrots as demand increases are also goods and services, the downward effects on the prices of those items will just offset the upward effect on the price of carrots. In this case, the price level, as an average, will be unaffected. But if what is given up is existing assets not counted in the price index, the rise in the price of carrots will not be offset by a fall in any other price in the price index and there will be a very slight degree of inflation. And though it is slight in this case, in other cases, when many more goods and services are involved, it is the only way inflation can occur.

It will be useful to consider the cases in which the increased willingness to buy carrots is financed by a willingness to give up money and bonds, rather than other goods. The money case is easiest because it's so obvious. Individuals maintain average levels of money balances based on factors to be considered later. The desired levels of money balances can be called demands for money. When actual money balances held are smaller than desired average holdings, individuals have shortages of cash. When money balances are temporarily greater than desired levels, individuals have cash surpluses.

In the carrot example, it is obvious that an increased demand for carrots financed by a willingness to reduce average money balances will not affect the prices of other goods and services—although there may be interest rate effects. The effect will be a tiny increase in the price level. This would be the standard inflation example.

A Possible Interest Effect

If, however, the increased demand for carrots is financed by a willingness to give up bonds, however improbable as a practical matter, the price level effect would not be the only effect. There would be a price level increase because the increased demand for carrots and the resulting price rise would not be offset by a fall in any other good or service price—in the short run. There would, however, be a fall, minor though it would be, in bond prices. A fall in bond prices would mean a rise in interest rates.

And all this just because a few people want more carrots. In the next chapter, we'll forget about carrots and concern ourselves with broader categories of economic values.

Chapter Two

How Different Markets Work

The economic mechanism of supply and demand governs every aspect of the economic process. But different markets are uniquely structured and depend on factors not necessarily common to other markets. The interest rate is an important factor in some markets, but is only indirectly involved in others. Likewise, the price level means one thing with respect to goods and services and another altogether with respect to asset holdings of money. Thus, each market must be discussed on its own terms. For convenience, this chapter will divide the economy into five basic markets. Each of these will be looked at in terms of basic characteristics and special factors.

In this context, the term "market" takes on a somewhat different meaning from its use in describing the carrot market of the previous chapter. There, a market was implicitly defined as a communications network through which the buying and selling of some specific product takes place. Here, markets will refer to categories of things rather than unique products. Each category will be designed to isolate portions of the economic process in which special factors are of significant importance. The five categories selected are: *goods and services,* or actual commodities being currently produced; *resource services,* or the rental use of human labor or physical equipment; *equities,* or ownership rights in productive resources (including common stocks and human capital in the form of learned skills and education); *bonds,* or financial obligations of both individuals and firms with fixed payment dates in the future (including personal notes); and *money,* or a class of assets including currency and commercial bank deposits. These will be considered in turn.

The Goods Market

The goods market covers the demand and supply process for all goods and services currently being produced. In the average college economics text, this is the only market that is adequately covered. Supply and demand interact to generate a per unit price for each good or service at which the quantity supplied equals the quantity demanded. If, at that price, there are above normal profits, new firms will enter the industry until such profits are eliminated. Likewise, if there are below normal profits at that price, firms will leave the industry until normal profits are restored. In the end, in the market for each individual product, the price will approach a level such that the profit level will be normal for the economy and that the quantity supplied equals the quantity demanded. Because this is well covered, there is little new here.

For the goods market as a whole, however, the price is more of a representative average of all goods and services. It is the price level itself. Just as one may speak of rising prices for food, one may speak of rising prices in general. That, of course, is the meaning of inflation. It is extremely important, however, to recognize the price level as a price itself just as the price of carrots is a price. The price level is not the price of everything one may buy in an economy. It is specifically the price that prevails for an average unit of output in the goods market. The price of common stocks and bonds and of labor in the form of wages are prices that may tend to rise when the price level rises, but these are not part of or the same thing as the price level.

When a market such as the goods market is spoken of, it is implicit that all goods and services are being added together. The supply of goods and services is the same as total output and that must somehow be measured in unit terms less descriptive and more mechanical than bunches of carrots. To add apples and oranges, one may speak of units of fruit. Fruit is less descriptive than apples or oranges, but it still conveys information in usage. Food is a further generalization that is even less descriptive than fruit. When one has reached the broadest level of generalization possible in the goods market, the term can be no more descriptive than a composite unit of goods and services.

That composite unit is based on statistical methods whose underlying logic is the amount of a representative basket of goods that could be bought with a dollar in some selected base year. In a price level index, that amount is set at 100 for the base year. In other years, the dollar will buy more or less of the composite unit of goods and services than it could in the base year. If a dollar will buy less, it will require more dollars to buy the composite unit of goods and services a dollar would buy in the base year. In that sense, its price will have risen and the price level number will be greater than 100. Likewise, of course, it will require fewer dollars that will buy more than a base year dollar to buy units of the composite unit and the price level number will be less than 100. Table 2-1 shows current figures for the price level. The term generally used for this is the *GNP Deflator*.

The price level, however, remains a normal price in the demand and supply sense. This must never be forgotten. If the general (aggregate) demand for goods and services in terms of dollars rises while the supply schedule remains unchanged, the

Table 2-1

Recent Price Level Figures *

YEAR	GNP DEFLATOR (price level)
1962	105.78
1963	107.17
1964	108.85
1965	110.86
1966	113.94
1967	117.59
1968	122.30
1969	128.20
1970	135.23
1971	141.61
1972	145.88

* Based on 1958 dollars.

price that is the price level must rise. Further, depending on what is happening in other markets, there may be increased output. If the general demand for goods falls while the supply schedule remains unchanged, the price level must fall and there may be reduced output.

What is different between the price level as a price and the price of carrots lies precisely in the supply response to changes in demand. Even this, however, is a matter of degree and not of kind. As was pointed out in the previous chapter, a change in the price of carrots must imply minute changes in other parts of the economy. These may to some extent offset the normal conclusion that a rise in the demand for carrots should produce both a rise in the price and in the quantity supplied of carrots. With carrots the extent is small. With goods and services as a whole, it's not so small. It may well be that concurrently with rising prices for goods there are rising prices for labor and other factors of production. If there are, the quantity supplied may remain constant as the price level rises. If there aren't, there will be an increased supply of goods and services and hence greater aggregate production.

28

Underlying the possibility that prices may rise while output is undisturbed is the notion that if costs of production rise as rapidly as prices, firms' profit margins will remain constant and there will be no incentive for them to increase output. This is common with prolonged inflation. However, at the outset of an inflationary period, the normal effect is that prices of goods are rising faster than costs of production, that firms do generate greater profits and that the increased output effect found in carrots is matched for goods and services as a whole. This will be returned to later. Here, it is only important to repeat that inflation must imply either an increased demand or a reduced supply of goods and services. There is nothing in the goods market that cannot be explained by the normal forces of supply and demand.

The Resource Services Market

The resource services market is normally treated in economic theory as simply the labor market. There are unique factors in the supply schedules for labor that are not true of the supply schedules for other resources, but concentration on these factors leads to more confusion than clarity. The *use* of resources and not merely their existence is required for production. The services of physical resources like plant and equipment is required in the same way as labor services. The demand for both kinds of resource services depends on the desire of firms to produce output for sale in the goods market.

What is different between labor services and the services of nonhuman physical resources is the way the resource involved is owned and what is given up in its use. The owner of physical resources may either be a firm or an individual, while the owner of human resources in a nonslave society must be the individual himself. What is given up in a decision to use a nonhuman resource at a particular time and place is the opportunity to use it at another time and place to earn an income. It may be used for one purpose or another or more or less intensively, each with different

implications for its durability, but the sole rationale for its ownership is normally the income that can be derived from its use.
This is not true of human resource potential. With human resources, leisure is given up by the seller and there is an important
tradeoff the owner must make between income and leisure—his
labor-leisure choice, discussed in the previous chapter.

The labor-leisure choice has the important implication that
theoretically a worker may, upon receiving a higher wage for his
labor, actually reduce the amount of it he is willing to sell. The
reason is that he may prefer to take some of the benefits his higher
income will afford him in the form of more leisure. If so, his
labor supply schedule has a *backward* portion and violates normal
supply schedule characteristics. If this is true of enough individuals, increased wages may actually cause a reduction in social
output. This is not true of nonhuman services where leisure is not
involved.

A second supply side difference between labor and the services of nonhuman resources *may* be greater downward rigidities
in wage adjustments than in downward adjustments in rental or
imputed rental (see below) prices of nonhuman resources. Falling
wages may be restrained by factors that do not restrain rental
prices from falling. Several reasons may be given for this. Workers may be less aware of changes in the price level than owners
of nonhuman resources. If so, they may suffer from "money illusion" and react only to money wages instead of real purchasing
power inherent in those wages. This means that workers may
resist downward money wage changes that would leave them no
worse off while other resource owners do not do this. Secondly,
the strength of labor unions and minimum wage laws may prevent the achievement of a lower price for labor at which quantity
supplied equals quantity demanded. Again, this is not true of
nonhuman resources.

The third difference between labor and nonhuman resource
services is apparent, but insignificant in terms of economic results.
This apparent difference exists between resources owned by a firm
and its labor supply. A firm need not own its resources, but fre-

quently does so. It could rent nonhuman resources from individuals or other firms just as it, in effect, rents its labor from individuals. But when it does not there is still an economic sense in which it rents its own resources to itself. This is the meaning of imputed rent. If a firm owns resources instead of renting them, it still gives up value in the process that closely parallels true rent. The easy way of looking at this is to observe that the firm could have rented the resources to some other firm. By using them itself, then, the firm gives up the rent it could have collected from other firms. The value of this rent that could have been collected is estimated as the imputed rent.

But with these clarifications, there is no essential difference between human and nonhuman resources. The market for each type of resource service, both human and nonhuman, is controlled by the supply and demand for each type.

The Equities Market

The equities market is the market for the *ownership rights* in resources. It includes both what is called human capital and equity shares in corporations of both common and preferred stock varieties as well as real estate, rental equipment and the like. Human capital is the word economists use for the value of acquired skills of individuals through education or experience. Different wages of different workers are explained by the different amounts of human capital they possess. A common stock is technically a fractional right in the physical plant and equipment of a corporation. Though the owner cannot claim his fractional share, what he owns is real and tangible. Real estate and tractors and other specific productive items are owned through deeds and titles. In each case, however, what is owned is resources whose value depends on productivity. This is the meaning of "real" in real assets, which is another term for equities. (Neither bonds nor money are "real" in this sense, as will be discussed below.)

The demand for equities is a demand for the flow of income these assets can be used to produce. The demand for education as a

31

financial venture (it may also be demanded for personal satisfaction) is a demand for the higher income that education will bring. The demand for common stock is a demand for dividends and rising stock prices that increase an individual's wealth over time. The demand for real estate is a demand for rent or for a higher future sale value. In each case, what is important to demanders is the rate of return, or the ratio between the rental or imputed rental return on the asset and its price. The rental returns are determined in the resource services market by the supply and demand for the services of the resource. The price of each asset is determined by the supply of and demand for ownership rights in that type of asset. These are separate supply and demand processes that are closely related through the interest rate.

To see how, consider an individual who is considering whether to invest $20,000 in either a bond or in a college education. Assume that he feels that his education will yield him an added average income of $1,000 per year for the next forty years of his life. Assume further that the prevailing interest rate on high grade bonds is 4.8 percent. In this case, the simple annual interest payment on the bond would be $960 per year. The education is a sound investment that would yield him $40 more per year than the bond. But if the interest rate had been 5.2 percent, the annual interest payment on the $20,000 bond would be $1040 per year and the education would be a poor investment in comparison to the bond. The same, of course, would have been true if the individual had been considering a common stock or a piece of real estate costing $20,000 that he expected to yield $1,000 per year.

Looked at in this way, the interest on high grade bonds is, in effect, the *economic cost* of investing in the education, stock or piece of real estate. The investment, at a price of $20,000, is a good investment only if the returns from the use of the asset are higher than the interest yield on the $20,000 bond. Only unwise investors would consider buying the equities at a price of $20,000 if the interest rate is 5.2 percent, but wise investors will be interested if the interest rate is 4.8 percent.

32

This means that the price of equities is regulated not only by the demand and supply for the services of assets, but also by the prevailing interest rate. The demand for such assets will take both factors into account. When the price of real assets is $20,000 and the interest rate is 4.8 percent, an investment will yield $40 more per year or .2 percent more than bonds. Put differently, an equity costing $20,000 that is expected to earn $2,000 per year has an expected rate of return of 5 percent. When risk factors are accounted for, as they implicitly are here in the notion of an average expected return, purchases of real assets are good investment decisions as long as the expected rate of return is at least as large as the prevailing interest rate on bonds. If it is not, investments in equities are not sound.

The supply of equities by other than speculators who gamble on everyday shifts in financial markets is composed of two parts. One part is the investors who, for one reason or another, want to sell their existing assets for current purchasing power (to pay for a long-awaited vacation perhaps) or in order to transfer into another type of investment (like bonds). The other part is firms who are in the business of manufacturing *new* producer goods for sale in the good market. As firms buy new producer goods, the underlying "real" holdings they have increase. And, as firms acquire more "real" holdings, the effective stock of equities increases.

Here again, however, the extent to which it makes sense to sell equities is governed by supply and demand in conjunction with the interest rate. Holders of existing equities will not try to switch out of their present holdings if they are earning attractive rates of return in comparison with the prevailing interest rate on bonds in the first part of the supply market for equities. In the second part, firms that are producing real assets will only increase their production if prices rise and profit margins increase.

Putting supply and demand together in the market produces the result that the demand for equities will be greater than the supply as long as the expected rate of return on real assets is greater than the interest rate on bonds. This is because a potential investor who can borrow at 4.8 percent and buy an equity yielding an expected return of 5 percent will tend to do so. In doing so, however, he will tend to bid up real asset prices relative to returns coming from the resource services market. This will cause the ratio, or rate of return, between asset returns and prices to fall.

He will also, in the process of borrowing, issue a personal note. This personal note is a type of bond and the issuance of such a note slightly increases the supply of bonds, causing the interest rate on bonds to rise slightly for reasons to be discussed when the bond market is considered. Thus, the rate of return on equities will tend to fall while the interest rate on bonds will tend to rise until both rates approach equality.

The Bond Market

In the bond market, the issues are similar to the equities market. There are two basic reasons why both firms and individuals borrow, thereby issuing bonds or notes or bills (all of which, again, are "bonds" in the sense of the economist). They may borrow purely in order to acquire current benefits. Individuals may borrow to have higher current standards of living. Firms may do the same thing in order to maintain high dividends with indirectly the same effect on stockholders. Firms and individuals may also borrow to act as financial intermediaries by using the borrowed funds to make investments with higher expected rates of return. In either case, the cost of borrowing to the borrower is the rate of interest that must be paid.

The interest rate reflects the future burden the borrower must bear for acquiring current benefits. The consumption borrower must have a lower standard of living in the future in order to have a higher standard of living in the present. The intermediary borrower has a future benefit to match his future cost and hopes to earn a net benefit for bearing the risk that he will, in fact, have a net loss. In either case, the interest rate is a measure of what is given up in a borrowing transaction.

The interest rate, however, exists in two senses and this is what is lost on many otherwise economically sophisticated persons. Many erroneous policy interpretations, including the Keynesian misinterpretation of the Great Depression, are based on a non-recognition of the dual nature of the interest rate. The problem is that inflation (and deflation during the Depression) is no stranger to the interest rate. The interest rate that is seen in the bonds market and discussed by monetary policy authorities is the *nominal* interest rate. "Nominal" means actual stated money terms independent of any inflationary or deflationary effect. But there is also a *real* interest rate that strips away the changes in the value of money that come with changes in the price level. The real interest rate is the value of the interest compensation or cost of bonds in terms of constant purchasing power. If nominal, or stated interest, is 7 percent and the continuing rate of inflation is 4 percent, the actual purchasing power difference is very close to 3 percent.

In terms of a lender or borrower, an *expectation* of 4 percent inflation will significantly affect the nominal, or money, rate of interest he would be willing to accept or pay. If an individual expects that inflation will be occurring over time, he will also expect that he will need more money in the future than now to accomplish any given future objective. In addition, he will expect that his future income will be higher and that the money he be required to back will involve less sacrifice than the value of the benefits he gets from money he receives now.

All this means that when both individuals have equal expectations about the rate of inflation (or deflation), they should be able to agree to an inflationary premium at this rate to the rate (the real rate) they would have been willing to accept with a stable level of prices. Thus, the difference between the nominal states rate of interest and the real rate is the *expected* rate of inflation. However, this *expected* rate and the *actual* rate of inflation may be entirely different. Expectations involve individual judgments about the future. Those judgments may well be wrong. If so, individual plans will be disrupted because their plans have been made on false premises. Some will gain unexpectedly and some will lose, but all will have readjustments to make on the basis of the difference between expected and actual outcomes. More will be said about this later.

The final special issue in the bonds market is the relationship between nominal interest rates and bond prices. Since bonds come in many denominations with many different systems of interest, payments, and maturity dates, economists have a special way of defining the price of bonds that strips away these differences. A *unit* of bonds is defined to be an amount of bonds big enough to yield $1 in simple interest in one year. The price of this amount of bonds is then used as the price of bonds. Thus, if the nominal interest rate is 5 percent, it would require $20 to buy a unit of bonds large enough to yield $1. At 10 percent, it would be $10. In application, this concept of bond prices can be used as follows: A $5,000 bond yielding 5 percent would be equal to 250 bond units priced at $20 per unit.

One other side advantage of this definition is that it can be seen immediately that higher bond prices imply lower interest rates and vice versa because the price of bonds is directly and inversely related to interest rates. This is, of course, well known to anyone who deals in financial markets, but not necessarily to all students of economics. The interest rate may be different for long- and short-term commitments, but for any given time span, it controls the prices of bonds of that period of duration. With these special considerations, it is again supply and demand that rule the bonds market. Each bond of each type of maturity date, procedure for varying interest, and size has its own market and a special price that accounts for these differences subject to the overall control of the interest rate.

The Money Market

In economic theory, the term "money market" has a different meaning from its use in financial circles. In financial circles, the term refers to the short-term bond market, but in economic theory it refers to the process by which demand and supply work on the financial assets that are money itself—commercial bank deposits of certain types to be discussed in the next chapter and currency in circulation. It is somewhat difficult to think in terms of "buying" money because it is the asset in terms of which all other things are "bought," but individuals do in fact demand more or less money, depending on its "price" in terms of purchasing power.

This market is special and crucial in the theory of monetarism. For that reason, the next chapter is devoted exclusively to that market. Yet, as in each other market discussed in this chapter, it is controlled by the forces of supply and demand. The primary difference between the money market and other markets lies in the way that money is supplied.

Chapter Three

The Role of Money

The money market, unique among all markets of the economy, has its supply side controlled by the monetary authorities of the Federal Reserve System. Other markets can be influenced by government policy and that is what is emphasized by Keynesian economists. There is no question that these other policies can have some effect on the economy, but the effects are minor in comparison with those exerted on the economy by monetary authorities on the supply of money. In Chapter 6, after the impact of changes in the supply of money have been completely analyzed, we will consider how the Federal Reserve System operates to control the money supply. In this chapter, we shall focus on the factors involved in the demand for money. With this focus, some of the issues involved on the demand side of the real assets, bonds and goods markets will be clarified.

Money as an Asset

What was lost on many economists before the twentieth century was the fact that money, in the final analysis, is a financial asset. To be sure, it is a unique asset because it serves as a *medium of exchange*. As a medium of exchange, money serves as the mechanism by which individuals trade among almost all other goods, services and nonmonetary assets. Individuals who want to sell their labor services in order to acquire goods and services do so by selling labor services for money (wages) and then use the money to purchase goods and services. Individuals who wish to trade bonds for stocks likewise normally sell the bonds for money that is then used to buy stocks. In each case, there are minor exceptions in which transactions go directly from labor to goods or bonds to stocks, but these are so rare in the American economy that they can be safely ignored. Thus almost every trade an individual (or firm) makes involves two transactions, going into and out of money. This medium of exchange role is central and obvious—so central and obvious that the asset role of money was long ignored, leading to many erroneous conceptions about the role of money.

The asset role of money derives from the fact that money can also be used as a *store of value*, perhaps better described by Milton Friedman as a *temporary abode of purchasing power*. In this respect, money can be used as a method of saving present purchasing power for the future. Few individuals or firms have same day cash flow operations in which a dollar is spent immediately after being earned. And since they do not, they hold purchasing power for some limited period of time in the form of money.

The form is, of course, important. Money as an asset has the important disadvantage of earning a very low rate of return or none at all. In times of inflation, this means that some forms of money actually earn a negative return. If inflation proceeds at 3 percent, money is losing value at a rate of 3 percent per year (if it earns no money yield). This is its real rate of return under such circumstances. However, this is only true of forms of money that have no offsetting yields. This is not always true. Certainly, it *is* true of currency stored in wallets or safety deposit boxes. It is also *apparently* true of demand deposits held as checking account balances, although not as true as it might seem on the surface. It is clearly *not* true of time deposits, or balances in savings accounts, held in commercial banks, which are counted as money by the supporters of the M_2 definition of money discussed in Chapter 1.

There are several reasons why it is only apparently true that demand deposits in checking accounts do not earn a rate of return. First, by servicing checks, banks serve an important record-keeping function for depositors. This record-keeping function has merit and constitutes a real return for depositors. Secondly, gifts of various sorts may be given to depositors for receipt of deposits of certain sizes. This is normally done on a gimmick basis, but it is a real return that should not be ignored. Third, and this is increasingly important under present inflationary conditions, banks competing for deposits have come up with several methods of circumventing laws preventing payment of interest on demand deposits.

One performed by a Chicago bank involves allowing the individual to set up a savings account and checking account concurrently. He may then run negative balances up to the limit of the balance in his savings account. The depositor owes no service charges on his negative balance in his demand account as long as he brings the balance up to zero at the end of each month. In the meantime, he continues to earn a money yield on his demand deposit held in the form of a time deposit. Other banks allow deficit accounts to be run as long as the balance is made positive at some level, say $200, at least once a month. This provides interest free loans at the latter part of the month, which is another real yield. Other banks have been evolving other gimmicks and it is clear that interest *would* be paid directly on demand account balances if this were not prevented by law.

The M_1–M_2 Controversy

The concept of money as an asset is important for properly understanding the dispute among economists over the M_1 and M_2 definitions of money. Money as a medium of exchange is directly used in the process of transactions. If the medium of exchange function is emphasized in defining money, the definition includes only those assets, namely currency and checkable bank deposits, that are used in actual payment. This definition is preferred by Keynesian economists who play down (but do not ignore) the store of value function of money. It is called the M_1 definition of money.

Monetarists, and especially Milton Friedman along with some economists of the Federal Reserve Bank of St. Louis, more strongly emphasize the store of value function of money in defining the money supply. They add time deposits (or savings account balances) in commercial banks to currency and checkable demand deposits. There are actually several reasons for this. First, as has been already seen, banks are and have been trying to find gimmicks to get around the legal restrictions against paying interest on demand accounts. As such, many of what look like savings account balances are actually restructured demand account balances. With this confusion, it is more consistent to simply include time deposits and thus avoid excluding time deposits that are in reality demand deposits.

Second, it is clear that rates paid on savings accounts are several percentage points below those on low-risk bonds. This lower rate points up the fact that savings account depositors are willing to accept a lower rate in order to have the advantages of savings account liquidity in preference to the higher rates and lower liquidity of bonds. Liquidity, in this sense, refers to the fact that savings account balances can be converted to cash easily at specified rates, while bond prices and hence interest rates are subject to fluctuations in the market. As such, the savings depositor can convert his deposits to cash without significant risk of loss or delay, while bondholders may find themselves having to take losses or else hold bonds to maturity.

This means that the individual who knows he will not need his money until maturity will prefer the higher rates on bonds while the individual who may want his funds before maturity dates will tend to prefer time deposits. Savings certificates, which combine characteristics of bonds and savings accounts, provide outlets for individuals who want a higher rate than exists on savings accounts, but are willing to give up more liquidity than simple savings depositors. Some savings certificates differ little from true time deposits, while others are virtually true bonds. The market, as in many other instances, provides a range of product types to meet every desired combination a saver might desire between yield and liquidity.

In reference to the definition of money, however, it is obvious that persons who are willing to accept the low rates on time deposits must feel some need for readily available funds. Long-*term* investors clearly do not choose time deposits because of low yields. But if only short term depositors choose time deposits, it is clear that time deposits serve Friedman's conception of a "temporary abode of purchasing power." Thus, emphasizing the store of value function of money leads quite naturally to the M_2 definition of money.

The case for the M_2 definition is also supported by Friedman and others by empirical studies that show that time deposits in commercial banks are, in fact, used in a money-like way. In this book, then, the discussion of money will be premised on the M_2 definition which, again, includes currency in circulation plus demand and time deposits.

The Concept of Portfolio Balancing

In order to fully understand the demand for money, it is necessary to understand the overall process by which individuals (and firms) plan their holdings of assets. This process is called portfolio balancing where "portfolio" means the total set of asset holdings of an individual (or firm) and "balancing" refers to the act of selecting a set of such assets that best fits the needs of the individual (or firm) doing the selecting.

As an individual plans his or his firm's portfolio of assets, he considers three basic factors—risk, liquidity, and money yield. An asset is more attractive if its risk is low, and its liquidity and yield are high. But since the demand and supply for each type of asset will reflect these factors, assets cannot be attractive in all three respects. If one was, its price would soon be bid up to the point that its yield as a ratio to its price would become low. Thus, there is clearly a tradeoff in practice between the advantages of low risk, high liquidity and high yield. No asset will have all three advantages and actual assets in the real world will exhibit varying degrees of each factor.

In terms of liquidity, assets range from currency on the one hand that is nearly 100 percent liquid to human capital on the other hand that cannot be sold and has zero liquidity. In terms of yield, assets range again from currency on the one hand that has no or a negative (real) yield to high speculative foreign investments that pay off handsomely if they work out but have a high probability of being total losses. In terms of risk, assets range from high-grade bonds of government issue to, again, highly speculative foreign investments.

As individuals choose assets, they consider a variety of factors including their ages, health, size of families, the types of gambling spirit they have and so forth. These are noneconomic factors. On the basis of these factors, they determine the degree of liquidity, yield and risk that best suits their needs. This indicates the type of portfolio they will seek in choosing assets and the amount of each asset they desire to hold. Then, within the portfolio, they will seek a combination of assets that will produce the desired level of risk, yield and liquidity.

In this, several things must be considered. There is a "pooling" effect on risk such that holding two assets of equal risk will produce a combination that is less risky than a simple holding of either. This is because the odds favor one doing better or worse than the other. If so, the outcome will be closer to the overall expectation that if only one such asset were held. Secondly, if an individual chooses one asset that is relatively liquid, he is less likely to accept other highly liquid assets. Only a certain amount of liquidity is needed by only one individual or firm. An individual can hold less money if he holds so-called *near money assets* like deposits in saving and loan associations and whole life insurance policies that can be borrowed against in emergencies—primary reason for wanting liquidity.

In a reasonably diversified portfolio, an individual will hold some real assets in the forms of both common stock and human capital, some monies and near monies and perhaps bonds. The amount of each type of asset, again, will depend on the amounts of others with similar characteristics and on the total size of the individuals' asset holdings. Money, in several forms, is one type of asset an individual is almost certain to hold. Some currency and at least one checking account with reasonable balances is a necessity although time deposits may be omitted if other assets that are reasonably liquid are held—similar deposits with savings and loan associations or mutual savings banks being obvious possibilities.

The Demand for Money

The demand for money can be easily seen in the context of the overall process of portfolio balancing. The demand for money is a demand for a highly liquid, low risk, low yield asset that can be used or easily converted to goods and services as a medium of exchange. It is a demand for a desired amount of such assets that, to be sure, will be higher at the beginning of a pay period than just before its end. Individuals routinely build up cash balances after receiving a paycheck, and then routinely draw them down as the period proceeds.

For this reason, the demand for cash balances is expressed in terms of average cash holdings. An individual who, for example, built up his cash balances to $700 at the beginning of a month and drew it down to $100 at its end would have an average balance of $400 over the month. It is also important to realize that as an individual is drawing down his balances, the firm he works for is building up its balances in anticipation of the next pay period. Thus, for society as a whole, the demand for cash balances tends to be stable, even while rising and falling for particular individuals and firms.

This overall demand is governed by a number of factors that will be considered in turn. Since the concept of average balances is being employed, these will be true both of individuals and of society as a whole. They are:

(1) Wealth at the beginning of the time period. The higher the total stock of wealth, the more consumer purchases most individuals will make and the larger their cash holdings are likely to be. This is true even though cash tends to be a smaller fraction of larger portfolios than small ones. Wealthy people tend to spend more money on transactions and need more money to handle them. This means that as wealth at the beginning of periods rise, the demand for cash balances will tend to rise.

(2) Income during a time period. Income, viewed as a monetarist would view it, is a flow of revenue from an individual's wealth over a time period. Wages and salaries are a flow of revenue from human capital, interest or returns from savings accounts are a flow from financial assets and rents and dividends are a flow from stocks, real estate and the like. In that respect, income is very much like wealth. The more income an individual earns, the more he will use for transactions and the more money he will need to handle them. Thus, like wealth, an increase in income will tend to lead to an increase in the demand for money balances.

(3) The price level. The price level determines the real purchasing power (or real balances) inherent in any given amount of money balances (and other wealth as well). This means that as the price level is higher, the amount of cash balances required to handle any given level of cash balances is larger. More money is

required to buy a given amount of items. Thus, as the price level rises, the demand for money balances will tend to rise.

(4) The interest rate. Interest is one measure of the cost of holding cash balances. Since a dollar held in cash balances is a dollar not held in an interest bearing form, the interest a dollar could have earned is an *opportunity cost* of holding money—something that is given up in a decision to hold money rather than bonds. The interest rate, however, works in the opposite direction from the first three factors. As the interest rate rises, the value of what is given up becomes greater—more interest is sacrificed. Since more is given up, the demand for cash balances will tend to fall. Thus, as the interest rate rises, the demand for money balances will tend to fall.

(5) The rate of return on equities. Like the interest rate, the rate of return available on forms of assets other than bonds is a factor in the demand for money. A dollar held as money is a dollar not held as equities just as it is a dollar not held as bonds. In the long run the rate of return on equities will tend to equal the interest rate, but in the short run this may not be true, which is the reason for treating it as a separate factor. However, the rate of return on equities works in exactly the same way as the interest rate. As it rises, more is given up by holding a dollar in the form of cash balances. Thus, as the rate of return on equities rises, the demand for cash balances tends to fall.

(6) The expected rate of inflation (or deflation if the rate is negative). This factor is perhaps hardest to understand because it works in the opposite direction from the changes in the price level it is based on. As the price level rises, more money is required to handle any given level of purchases. But, at the same time, an expected rising price level means that an individual believes that every dollar he holds is losing purchasing power at a rate equal to the expected rate of inflation. This means that instead of zero or a low positive yield, money as an asset is yielding a negative amount. The force of this factor is to reduce the amount of cash balances an individual desires to hold.

This can perhaps be better understood if a careful distinc-

47

tion between real and nominal money balances is made. Parallel-ing the earlier discussion of real and nominal factors, nominal cash balances are simply the number of dollars held. Real balances are the amount of purchasing power contained in the nominal balances. As the price level rises in an expected fashion, an individual will need a larger amount of nominal balances to handle his transactions. But, at the same time, the individual faces a negative yield on every dollar he holds and will try to get by on a smaller volume of real purchasing power in money than in a non-inflationary situation. This means that while nominal balances increase with any type of inflation, real balances will be reduced with expected inflation. More simply, nominal balances will be increased less than in proportion to the rising price level when inflation is expected.

In summary, then, an increase in the expected rate of inflation will tend to reduce the demand for nominal money balances. It is a factor that increases the opportunity cost of holding money and must be added to the interest rate or the rate of return on real assets to calculate the true cost of holding money.

Adjustments in the Money Market

Having carefully considered the factors that determine the demand for money, the conditions for full adjustment in the money market can be established. The supply of money is a constant, determined by monetary authorities. The supply side of the market is therefore not free to react to market forces. Therefore, the market must adjust itself by changes in the demand for money. To see how this happens, it will be useful to consider situations in which the demand for money is greater than and less than the existing money supply.

If, for whatever reason, the demand for cash balances exceeds the existing money supply, there will be a shortage of money to meet demand. Individuals will attempt to solve their personal parts of this shortage in several ways. First, they may try to sell other assets in order to acquire more money. As they do so, the quantity supplied of these assets will increase (along with other effects it will be useful to defer until the next chapter). The increase in the quantity supplied of other assets will cause their prices to fall. And as asset prices fall, their rates of return—the interest rate and the rate of return on equities—will rise. These rates, as has just been seen, are factors whose rise causes the demand for money balances to fall. Thus, as individuals attempt to sell other assets in order to acquire money balances, they affect changes in the markets for these assets that, in turn, decrease the demand for money. This process, with resulting decreases in the demand for money balances, will continue until full adjustment occurs in the money market. It stops only when the demand for money has fallen to the point that the quantity demanded of cash balances equals the money supply.

It is, however, not the only reason that the demand for money falls when the demand for money exceeds the money supply. The second reason is that indirectly (and perhaps to a lesser extent directly), the attempt by individuals to acquire more money balances will reduce the quantity demanded of goods and services. The precise nature of how this happens depends on why the demand for money exceeds the money supply. This will be discussed later. For now, it is only important to note that shortages of cash balances will ultimately cause individuals to reduce the quantity of goods and services they demand. This, again, will leave a variety of effects to be considered later. But among them will be a downward pressure on the price level. This downward pressure on the price level, whether the price level actually falls or merely stops rising as rapidly as before, will reduce the demand for money in the way discussed earlier in the chapter.

Clearly, then, there are several consequences of an attempt by individuals to acquire cash balances that will ultimately reduce their demands for money balances. This will continue until the demand for money has fallen to the point at which the demand for money equals the money supply, thus establishing full adjustment in the money market.

If the initial situation had been that the demand for money was smaller than existing money supply, the effects would have run in exactly the opposite directions. The attempt to use excess money to buy other assets would result in a rise of their prices and hence a fall in their rates of return. This then causes the demand for money to increase. Again, the process continues as long as the demand for money continues to be smaller than the money supply. Likewise, ultimately and for reasons to be considered later in detail, the excess supply of money will lead to an increased demand for goods and services. This, among other things, will cause an upward pressure on the price level. And, in turn, the upward pressure on the price level will cause an increase in the demand for money, again continuing as long as the money supply exceeds the quantity demanded of money.

The Price of Money

The final topic in understanding the role of money is to specify precisely the price of money. If demand and supply are at work, there must be a price that can adjust upward or downward. That price in the case of money is the inverse of the price level. The reason is as follows. The price of a thing is the amount of what must be given up *directly* to acquire it. Since most things are acquired through money, their prices are expressed in terms of the amount of money that must be given up to acquire one unit of the thing—be it an hour of labor, a share of common stock, a bond, or a carrot. In the case of money itself, however, money is not used to buy money in the sense of acquiring a different thing through purchases. Instead, money is acquired by giving up things—labor, goods, stocks or bonds—to acquire money. Therefore, the price of money in some way is expressed in terms of "things."

The most general concept of "things" other than money in which the price of money could be expressed is the basket of "things" on which the price level is based. This basket is composed of a cross section of all goods and services and is defined in such a way that one base year dollar (presently the 1967 dollar) would just buy it. The price of money can be best expressed in terms of the number of units of such baskets it takes to buy one dollar of money. Clearly in the base year, the price of money is one because it takes one real dollar's worth of things to buy the dollar of that year. In later years, it will be one divided by the price level, which will express the number of real dollar's worth of things that it takes to buy any given year's dollar. Hence, the price of a dollar is the inverse of the price level.

This has a final implication worth noting. Since the price level is the overall price of goods and services and the inverse of the price level is the price of money with both markets reacting to the forces of supply and demand, it is obvious that the price level is determined in both the money and goods markets and not in the goods market alone.

Milton Friedman, once asked to succinctly define monetarism, replied, "Money matters."

Chapter Four

When Money is Added

In this chapter, the actual theory of monetarism begins. The previous chapters have had a monetarist slant, but they have been basic to any reasonable theory of economic changes. One could, in fact, develop a completely Keynesian theory from those chapters although that's not what is done by Keynesians. There are many theories that could fit the truths of the applications of supply and demand to the basic markets of the economy. Monetarism is only one such theory, but it has two things working hard on its behalf. For one thing, it's the most reasonable theory in terms of common sense intuition. For another, there's considerable empirical evidence, compiled by Milton Friedman and others, to suggest that it's consistent with the historical record.

It is not the purpose of this book to review the historical record except to make particular points and to answer specific questions. That has been well handled elsewhere.* Instead, the focus is on the internal logic of the theory—the explanation of the sequence of events that leads naturally and inevitably to monetarist conclusions. These can be stated easily in advance. The basic monetarist conclusion is that changes in the supply of money are the most important single source of economic fluctuations in the economy—the primary source of both inflations and recessions. Changes in the money supply are not the *only* source of economic fluctuations in monetarist theory, as has been sometimes charged by opponents, but it is far and away the most important source.

Monetarism is largely a theory of the effects of changes in the money supply. The nature of these effects depends in a very specific way on what has been happening in the economy prior to the changes that occur in the money supply. This will all be covered in the next two chapters. The effects that derive from a change in the money supply in either direction proceed through a long and involved process that is moderately complicated because so many things are happening and not because any one of those things is difficult. To proceed carefully and clearly, it will be useful to consider first the effects of adding money to the economy or adding money faster than before and then, in the next chapter, the effects of reducing money or adding money slower than before.

The Initial Assumptions

Economists are fond of talking about model building and there is a common reaction by others that the models they build are not applicable to anything but the ivory tower economic journals in which they are published in Greek letter equations. There is much truth to this criticism, but, at the same time, it should not be carried to the extreme of resistance to all levels of abstraction. The proper function of model building is that of simplifica-

* See especially Milton Friedman and Anna Jacobson Schwartz, *A Monetary History of the United States, 1867-1960* (Princeton: Princeton University Press, 1963), and A. James Meigs, *Money Matters: Economics, Markets, Politics* (New York: Harper and Row, 1972).

tion and it is used that way here. A model is nothing more than a set of simplifying assumptions that can be explained in either words or equations. The simplifications made here are technically a "model" in that sense, but they will all be relaxed by the end of the chapter. Much in the way of clarity will be gained in the process and nothing in the way of realism will be lost because the relaxation of assumptions will return the discussion gradually to real world conditions.

These are initial simplifying assumptions: (1) that for several years prior to the changes that will be introduced in the money supply, the price level has been stable and constant so that no expectations of inflation exist; (2) that the rate of real economic growth is zero in the long run so that a stable price level has been produced by a constant money supply (for reasons to be explained later); (3) that international economic effects are so minimal as to be ignored; and (4) that the period prior to introduced changes in the money supply was one of full economic adjustment in all markets so that extraneous considerations can be ignored.

Into this temporarily unreal world an increase in the money supply will be introduced. How this happens will be explained fully in Chapter 6. Here, only its consequences will be analyzed. The first consequence is simple and direct. Since the demand for money just equaled the money supply at its original level, the newly created money will necessarily mean that, until something else happens, the demand for money will be smaller than the new larger money supply. Normal market forces begin to operate. Individuals have excess money in terms of their overall portfolio considerations and try to use it to acquire other things they want more than cash balances.

Price Level Effects

At this point, it will be useful to divide further discussion in terms of specific objectives. Before considering the changes that occur in each market independently, it will be useful to get an over-

55

view of the entire process. This can be done most clearly by looking first at the process by which the price level changes and then
at the process by which the real production of goods and services
changes. When that is done, it will be fairly simple to return to
each of the five basic markets of the economy in order to tie up
loose ends.

Following the increase in the money supply, individuals first
turn to the asset markets to acquire income-yielding assets with
excess money. Bonds, in this respect, are somewhat more attractive
than most types of real assets because of the lower risk involved in
immediate purchases at a time when individuals had not been
previously planning new investments. This has the important investment consequence that rising bond prices will occur somewhat
before rising equity prices, but over several months following the
increase in the money supply, the demand for both bonds and
equities will be rising. The increased demand will cause asset
prices to rise.

As asset prices rise, two things happen. First, both interest
rates and rates of return on equities fall. In the case of bonds,
this has to be the case since rising bond prices directly imply
falling interest rates. In the case of equities, it happens because
nothing has yet happened to affect the returns on equities. Since
returns on real assets are unchanged and their prices have risen,
it is clear that the rate of returns on the assets must fall. These
are the price effects of the increased demand for assets resulting
from an excess supply of money in the money market.

There are also effects on the quantity supplied of assets.
Again, it is important to remember that *everything* in economics
can be boiled back into supply and demand forces interacting in
various markets. The increased demand for assets both causes
the price of assets to rise *and* increases the quantities of assets that
"producers" are willing to supply. "Producers" is in quotation
marks because the supply situation is relatively unique in the case
of bonds although more conventional in the case of equities.

The suppliers of bonds are borrowers—both individuals and
firms—who issue promises to pay in the future in return for in-

creased purchasing power in the present. As the price of bonds rises and the interest rate of bonds consequently falls, it becomes cheaper to borrow and both firms and individuals begin to borrow more, thereby increasing the quantity supplied of bonds. In the case of real assets, new real plant and equipment on which the "realness" of real assets is based begins to be produced when prices rise by firms operating according to normal profit motivations in the production process.

The greater ease of borrowing in the bonds market, of course, facilitates purchases of investment goods as a process of increasing the supply of real estate. It also has a further consequence in terms of consumption. In terms of monetarist theory, a fall in the reward for saving and the necessarily corresponding cost of dissaving will mean that individuals will save less and consume more of their incomes. Thus, both the investment and consumption demands for goods and services rise.

This, in turn, means that the prices of goods and services begins to rise and with them, of course, the price level. Thus does an increase in the supply of money transmit itself into a higher price level.

Real Output Effects

The movement of demand from market to market does not stop with the goods market. It moves on through the quantity supplied effects of increases in the demand for goods and services. Because prices have risen while costs of production have not yet been affected, firms' profit margins rise and they attempt to increase their real output of goods and services. This attempt, then, transmits the increase in demand into the resource services market. More resource services are needed to produce the additional output.

As the demand for resource services to produce additional output increases, wages and rents begin to rise in money terms. What must be recognized, however, is that the *real* value of wages

57

and rents is now lower than it was before the increase in the money supply. This is because prices of goods and services have risen sooner and faster than wages and rents. Since this is true, the real purchasing power of wages and rents has fallen. The market responds in a relatively unique, but obvious way.

Since the quantity supplied of resource services would only increase in response to standard pricing procedures if the real wages and rents had risen, the only way firms can get a larger input of labor and, to a lesser extent, capital is to offer overtime pay and equivalents. This creates a situation in which wages paid on the standard workweek are lower in real terms than before the increase in the money supply, but wages paid for hours worked beyond the standard workweek are significantly higher. Overtime pay becomes common and the economy enters a "true boom" stage, or a period of overproduction. Another effect is that workers have not yet become accustomed to thinking in terms of dollars with less purchasing power. If so, there may be a temporary "money illusion" during which workers perceive rising money wages as rising real wages in spite of the opposite reality. Such an effect might cause workers to offer more labor even in the absence of overtime inducements.

It is not customary to think of overproduction as an economic problem, but rather as a blessing. This is somewhat myopic. When workers are induced to provide more than a normal labor input, they gradually become exhausted and when the boom condition disappears, there is a tendency for workers to take more sick leave, longer vacations and to provide more slack effort. Likewise, machines that are overused during a boom begin to break down sooner and their repair-time loss contributes to the slack in production that is almost sure to follow the boom. A temporary increase in real output during boom periods may well result in a long-run decline in production through the future slack it inherently creates.

Be that as it may, the boom condition of the economy is not stable. As long as it exists, firms will have an incentive to compete among themselves for more labor in order to reduce the overtime component in their labor forces. As long as increased overtime persists, then there will be upward pressure on wages and rents in proportion to the initial rise in prices.

As wages and rents rise, firm costs of production also increase, gradually catching up with the initial revenue increases inherent in higher prices. As this happens, profit margins return to initial levels and the quantity of resource services declines back to approximately its initial level. Increased overtime disappears and real output falls back to a lower real level than before the increase in money as the slack caused by prior overproduction begins to take its toll. If no further disturbances occur the economy then gradually restores itself to initial real output pattern.

This completes the overview. Now, the individual markets will be considered, beginning with the money market.

The Money Market

The chain of events following an increase in the money supply begins, of course, in the money market itself with an initial excess supply of money. As individuals attempt to move out of money into other assets and eventually into goods, there are three different factors that operate to increase the demand for money. Only one of these is permanent, but the temporary impact of the other two supports the restoration of equilibrium in the money market.

The attempt to use money to buy assets, as has been seen, leads to higher asset prices and both a lower interest rate and a lower rate of return on equities. The declines in these two rates are the temporary factors in the restoration of full adjustment in the money market. By the end of the total adjustment process, they will return to approximately their initial levels. But while they are temporarily lower, they have the effect of increasing the demand for money. As discussed in the previous chapter, the interest rate and the rate of return on real assets are both opportunity costs of holding money. When they fall, then the demand for money will increase. Thus, during the part of the process that

59

these rates are temporarily lower, they have an upward effect on the demand for money.

Even at the early stages of the adjustment process, the money demand effects of lower asset yields are supported by the beginning rise in the price level in the good market. The price level is another factor in the demand for money and, as the price level rises, the demand for money will be subject to upward pressure. Thus, in the early stages of the general adjustment process, there are three different reasons why the demand for money will be increasing— the fall in the interest rate, the fall in the rate of return on real assets, and the rise in the price level. The money market will approach a state of quasi-full adjustment when the upward pressure of these factors is strong enough that the demand for money approaches the level of the supply of money.

This, however, is only apparently a stable situation. As the process of adjustment proceeds, the interest rate and the rate of return on real assets will begin to return to their initial values. Since this means that they are falling, this will constitute a downward pressure on the demand for money. This downward pressure, however, will be more than offset by the upward pressure of the continuing rise in the price level. Gradually, the money market will reach true full adjustment.

In the end the money market will show an increase in demand proportionate to the money supply, and the technical price of money, the inverse of the price level, will be lower. This is because with a higher price level the purchasing power of each dollar will be lower.

The Bonds Market

Changes in the bonds market begin with attempts to use excess money to buy bonds. This increases the demand for bonds and the resulting shortage of bonds causes both a price rise and, over the longer term, a gradually increasing supply of bonds. The price effect is much more immediate than the effect on quantity supplied.

The price of bonds rises and their interest rates correspondingly fall. This is the obvious effect at the early part of the adjustment process.

As this occurs, however, it becomes cheaper for both firms and individuals to borrow. The interest they must pay to borrow is lower. Therefore, the rate of borrowing begins to increase, gradually increasing the total number of bonds available in the economy. This gradual increase in the supply of bonds will, as is normal for an increase in supply in any market, have a gradual downward effect on bond prices that slowly reverses the original rise. The quantity of bonds supplied continues to increase until the price of bonds returns approximately to its initial level. When it has, interest rates will also have returned to their initial approximate levels.

In the end, however, though bond prices have risen and then returned to initial *nominal* values, the *real* value of each unit of bonds is permanently lower. Those who have held bonds throughout the adjustment process are worse off because the money they will be paid back will purchase fewer goods and services than the money they lent. From society's standpoint, however, the total stock of bonds will have the same real value as before the increase in the money supply. The *nominal* amount of bonds will be greater than it was initially because of the number of new bonds issued during the general adjustment process, but the number of bonds will have increased in approximate proportion to the loss in value of each initial bond. Thus, if the overall fall in the price level was 3 percent each bond will be worth 3 percent less in real terms than it was before the increase in the money supply. But, at the same time, the total number of units of bonds in the economy will have increased by approximately 3 percent so that the total real value of bonds will be the same as initially.

The Equities Market

As in the case of bonds, the initial impact of the increase in the money supply is a rise in the prices of equities. This lags slightly behind the rise in bond prices, but is caused by the same forces involved in the rise in bond prices. When equity prices rise, their returns have been as yet unaffected and hence rates of return fall.

The increased demand also has the quantity supplied effect that profits increase in industries producing the real factors of production on which equities are based, and so these industries produce more output and hence more equity. This rise in the quantity supplied of equities, however, does not continue throughout the adjustment process and certainly does not ever offset the price rises in equities as happens in the case of bonds. This is because indirect returns on equities in the form of wages and rents soon begin to rise in proportion to the initial rise in asset prices. As this happens, costs of production in producer good industries go up and their output returns to initial levels. These returns continue to rise until the initial rate of return is restored. Thus, at the end of the adjustment process, equity prices—unlike bond prices—will be permanently higher, but their rates of return will have returned to initial levels. Investors who hold equities through the entire adjustment process will tend to have neither gained nor lost purchasing power at its end.

From the standpoint of society as a whole, it is possible that the total stock of resources will have risen. This, however, must be seen in the context of the fact that the boom portion of the adjustment process will have caused some resources to wear out early. The net effect may be either a reduction or an increase in the total stock of resources. The change could be in either direction, but is not likely to be large in either case.

The Goods Market

The initial impact on the goods market arises both from the increase in consumer demand and from an increase in investment demand. The increased consumer demand is caused by lower interest rates and rates of return on real assets. Since the reward for saving is lower, there is greater incentive for individuals to enjoy a higher standard living in the present. Likewise, when loans are cheaper, individuals are more likely to borrow to increase their holdings of real assets. Thus, on both consumption and investment fronts, the demand for goods and services increases in response to lower interest rates.

This increase in demand causes the prices of goods and services and therefore also the overall level of prices to rise. It also increases profit margins of firms on a temporary basis. Firms, attempting to capitalize on temporarily higher profit margins, attempt to produce more output. Output does increase. To do this, however, they must acquire more resource inputs. In attempting to acquire more resource inputs, firms react in two ways. First, they attempt to get more resource service output from their present holdings of equipment and other physical resources and from their existing labor forces. Second, they attempt to hire more labor and to either rent or purchase more nonhuman resources.

In both cases, the general impact is rising costs of production. Machines and other equipment that are used more intensively begin to have higher repair costs. Workers must be paid overtime to supply more labor. And, as new resources and more labor are bid for, their prices begin to rise. These rises, of course, begin to offset initially higher profit margins. As rising costs begin to catch up with rising prices, firms will return to initial production levels and the overall level of production recedes back toward its initial level. For a short period of time after this, output will even tend to go below its initial level as machines that were overutilized are repaired and workers who were working overtime begin to take more sick leave and longer vacations. Eventually, this effect dissipates and the level of production finally returns to normal.

At this point, both prices and costs of production will have risen in proportion, as have profit margins. Money profits will be higher in nominal terms, but the *rate* of profit will be the same as it was initially. *Real* profits will be no higher than before, both in terms of dollars and as a rate.

The Resource Services Market

The last market to be affected by an increase in the money supply is the resource services market. In that sense, unions are correct in complaining that President Nixon's wage and price controls operated to the benefit of corporations and at the expense of labor. Wage and price controls attempted (fortunately with not much success) to freeze the normal adjustment process at a stage at which price rises had progressed further than wage rises.

By the time that inflation spreads to the labor market *and* the market for the services of nonhuman resource services, prices of other things have already risen. Thus, the real wages of resources have fallen at this point. Because of inherent rigidities in patterns of resource employment, there will not have been a reduction in the amount of resource services offered for employment, but the standard of living of workers will have temporarily become lower in real terms. Because, by assumption, there was relative full employment at the outset, the beginning of the increase in demand for resource services cannot actually increase the supply of resource service offerings by a normal pricing method. Not until wage rises had caught up with price rises would workers supply more labor if normal pricing were employed. And even then, if the labor supply schedule has a backward bend, it would not.

What is done is a different pricing tactic by firms—overtime offerings at time and a half or double time. When overtime is offered, a firm is in effect saying to the worker: if you will work 40 hours (or 35) at one rate, we will pay you a much higher rate for any additional hours you work. This gets around the problem that real wages have fallen for the standard work week because overtime pay means that *marginal* wages have risen in both real and nominal terms. The parallel situation with nonhuman resources is not generally overtime rents (or imputed rents), but rather the much higher maintenance costs that go with rates of overutilization.

The overtime-higher maintenance cost situation is, however, unstable. Firms that are paying overtime have an incentive to try to acquire more resources in order to eliminate the overtime component of their wage bills. Likewise, they try to hire or purchase more nonhuman resources to reduce their per unit maintenance costs. Thus, in both cases, as long as there is overutilization, demand by firms for more resources will continue until wages and rents rise in proportion to prices. And as that happens, the initial rise in profit margins that caused firms to demand more resources in the first place will disappear. Overtime offerings will then cease and rates of utilization of nonhuman resources will return to normal.

This, again, will be followed by a period during which resources—both human and nonhuman—will go through periods of recovery. Workers will take more time off and postponed machine services will be done, with the effect that resource service offerings will fall during the recovery period. This period will end when recovery is complete.

Adjustment with Growth

This completes the discussion of the adjustment process in the simplest possible situation—a situation with no growth, no inflationary expectations, no international complications and beginning at a point of full economic adjustment. What will happen when full adjustment is not the initial situation is covered in the process of discussing various stages of the adjustment processes in this chapter and the next, so that requires no special treatment at this point. However, the other three simplifying assumptions need to be relaxed. The assumption of no real economic growth will be the first unrealistic simplification to be eliminated.

All modern developed economies grow. Indeed, that is part of the definition of a "developed" economy. Real economic growth occurs when society chooses to progressively increase the number of productive resources it possesses as time goes by. This, however, implies that the members of society are willing to forego some amount of present consumption for the purpose of acquiring a better standard of living in the future. In this respect, the process of growth begins with individual choices between consumption and saving as discussed in Chapter 1. Saving is not always smoothly converted into income-earning and output producing resources, but without more saving, there will not be more resources. Saving above the amount necessary to replace depreciating resources is necessary for the growth of an economy, just as for a firm.

The choices of individuals between consumption and saving (or, more clearly, between consumption and future income) tend to form stable patterns in most societies and the United States is no exception. This pattern tends to produce a rate of increase in resources that is relatively stable, although not necessarily constant, in the long run. For example, a rate of growth that slowly but consistently rose from 4 to 5 percent over a 30-year period would be stable, but not constant. The rate in the United States has tended to fluctuate in the range of 2 to 6 percent with an average between 3 and 4.

If growth patterns are stable in the long run, it is possible to conceive a more dynamic form of the adjustment process for the effects of *relative* monetary increases. In this process, the demand and supply schedule in most markets will tend to be increasing at rates similar to the rate of growth. Growth clearly manifests itself on the supply sides of three of the five markets of the economy—the equities market where there are more productive resources; the resource services market where there are more potential resource hours of inputs; and the goods market in which there are more goods and services.

Just as obviously, the process of increasing supplies has the effect of increasing demands in all of the markets in a stable predictable fashion. As more resource services are supplied, individuals earn larger real incomes and demand more goods and services, equities and bonds. Firms, of course, must demand more resources services in order to produce more output and must issue more bonds in order to purchase more resources of the nonhuman variety. These same forces operate on the demand side of the money market, at least in terms. Individuals and firms, with larger

66

real incomes and larger volumes of transactions, need larger amounts of real money balances to handle them.

The supply of money is another question. Its control does not rest with market forces, but rather with authorities of the Federal Reserve System. If they do not permit the money supply to expand while supplies and demands in all other markets, including the demand for money, are expanding, it will remain constant. But, if the money supply does remain constant while the demand for money is increasing, the price of money will rise—the normal market outcome. The price of money, as mentioned earlier, is the inverse of the price level and the way the price of money rises is by a falling price level. This is intuitively obvious since the same amount of *nominal* money is being spent on more goods and services. It is to be expected that the prices per unit of goods and services would fall and they would. The impact of a constant money supply under conditions of economic growth would be a falling price level. This happened, with some modification, from the end of the Civil War to 1900 in the United States.

An obvious implication, however, is that if Federal Reserve authorities choose instead to allow the money supply to increase at the same rate as the rate of growth in the output of goods and services or slightly faster (see below), the price level will not fall in this way. This, in general, is the basic policy prescription of monetarism.

It is not quite true, however, that the demands and supplies in all markets increase in proportion as growth occurs. Some will grow slightly faster and some slightly slower than the general growth rate. In particular, the demand for money has increased somewhat faster. This may happen because money is something of a luxury good in the sense that as people become more wealthy, they tend to hold relatively larger amounts of real money balances. This is because as people become more wealthy, they can afford to keep more cash in reserve for emergencies. Until the 1950s, when some of the emergency functions of money were taken over by credit cards, the demand for money had been increasing slightly faster than the growth rate throughout the portion of American history for which data exist.

If, then, the demand for money increases slightly faster than the rate of increase in goods and services, the price level would fall slightly if the money supply increased only as rapidly as goods and services. In order to maintain a constant price level, the supply of money should be increased slightly faster than the rate of growth. This, however, may only be an historical consideration. Since the middle 1950s, the demand for money has been increasing at a slightly slower rate than the rate of growth. This is due, among other reasons, to the extensive development of credit cards since that time. There are reasons for believing that the long-run trend of a more rapidly increasing demand for money will eventually reassert itself, but this remains to be seen.

The reason for the credit card effect is that one of the main advantages of money has been the precautionary value of money, stemming from its liquidity. Individuals desire to have purchasing power on hand to cope with emergencies. The existence of credit cards means that purchasing power is more easily available in the form of credit if emergencies arise and less money itself is needed for this purpose.

In any case, the dynamics of growth imply that changes are going in all markets in a relatively stable way. If, in such a situation, the supply of money is the only supply or demand force not to change, the price of money must increase and the price level of goods and services must fall.

The Rate of Expectations

The second initial assumption to fall is that there are no expectations of changes in the price level. It is clear that the price level has not always been stable in the past—and that is a gross understatement. From 1865 to 1900, the price level fell at a rate of approximately 1 percent per year. From 1965 to the present, it has been rising at a rate between 3 and 5 percent per year. Both individuals and firms were aware of these conditions in both cases.

The fact that individuals come to develop expectations that the price level will change over time brings into play another crucial factor in several markets. This factor, the expected rate of change in the price level, was discussed with reference to both the bonds and money markets in chapters 2 and 3, but was assumed out of existence in the discussion of an expansion of the money supply in this chapter. It can actually be separated into two parts: the actual average expected rate of change and the degree of uncertainty about the accuracy in that rate. These will be considered in turn.

To simplify the discussion of the expected rate of change in the price level (either inflationary or deflationary), it will be useful to assume that there is a fair degree of confidence that the existing rate will be maintained. And, to be realistic in the discussion, it will be assumed that the rate is positive so that it is an expected rate of inflation. Specifically, if the rate of inflation for the past four years has been consistently close to 3 percent, there is reason to suppose that individuals and firm managers will expect that the rate for the next few years will also be 3 percent.

With this condition in existence, it is obvious from what has been said before that the supply of money has been increasing slightly more than 3 percent more per year than the rate of real economic growth. For example, if the rate of increase in goods and services has been consistently increasing at 4 percent and the money supply has been increasing at slightly more than 7 percent, the price level will be increasing at a rate of 3 percent.

Given that this has been happening for some time, individuals and firms will have adjusted their plans to include the expectation that it will continue to happen in the future. If, as expected, it does happen that way, the adjustment process for an increase in the money supply—described earlier in this chapter—will not occur, simply because the money supply is increasing. What will happen is another version of full economic adjustment.

Because individuals and firms expect the price level to be increasing at a rate of 3 percent, they expect their nominal balances to be losing purchasing power at a rate of 3 percent per year. And, as such, they will be expecting to have to increase their cash holdings by 3 percent just to maintain constant real balances. Further, because their real incomes are rising at 4 percent because of economic growth, they will be increasing cash balances by another 4 percent to cover these transactions. Thus, the demand for nominal balances will be increasing at a rate of 7 percent to just match the corresponding rise in the money supply. With this occurring, the money market will remain in a type of dynamic full adjustment. At each point in time, demand will equal supply and there will be no spread of effects to other markets.

However, other effects based on the expected rate of change in the price level will be occurring in the other markets. In the bonds market, both borrowers and lenders understand that money that will be paid back will be worth 3 percent less in purchasing power than money loaned in the present. Lenders will demand higher rates than if this were not the case and borrowers will be willing to pay them. Essentially, both borrowers and lenders will be able to agree to nominal or actual money rates that are 3 percent higher than the rates they would have been willing to agree to when the price level was expected to be constant. Thus, the expected rate of inflation will reflect itself in the bonds market as an inflationary premium added to the real interest rate.

In the real assets market, both resource returns and asset prices will be rising in proportion so that, viewed in one way, the rate of return on real assets at any point in time remains constant. This rate continues to be approximately equal (or it may be a little lower, depending on just how the money supply was increased— see Chapter 7) to the initial real rate of interest. Viewed over time, however, the increases in the prices of real assets are part of the returns to their owners. When this value appreciation is counted as part of the rate of return, its nominal value is equal to the nominal interest rate and the expected rate of inflation is reflected by the rate of price rises in real assets.

In the goods market, of course, the expected rate of inflation is reflected by the actual rate of inflation. Likewise, in the resource services market, with full adjustment to an expected rate of inflation, nominal wages and rents will be rising in proportion to the price level. The real wage rate will thus be constant. Thus, in every market, a full adjustment situation is in evidence and, as long as expectations of inflation continue to be justified by actual experience, no readjustment is necessary.

When Expectations are Not Realized

When expectations are not realized, however, individual and firm planning will be disrupted. Here, we return to a process similar to that discussed in the initial highly simplified version of the effects of changes in the money supply. Until we have the analysis of the next chapter, it will be useful to postpone discussion of the impact when the rate of inflation is less than the expected rate of inflation. Here, the discussion will center on the impact of a rate of inflation greater than that expected. This impact will be almost identical to the impact of an increase in the money supply when there has been no growth and a previously constant price level. Since the process is so similar, the discussion will be much more abbreviated than the original discussion.

In the money market the demand for money will be increasing at a rate based on previous experiences and expectations about the future. In the specific example used before, if the money supply has been increasing slightly faster than 7 percent, with 4 percent growth and a rate of inflation of 3 percent, the demand for money will be increasing at 7 percent per year. If the money supply unexpectedly begins to increase faster than that, the initial impact will be an undesired buildup of cash balances and an excess supply of money. If, for example, the supply of money began increasing at 9 percent, the supply would be rising slightly less than 2 percent more rapidly than demand is increasing (slightly less because, in the example, the supply was increasing initially slightly *more* than 7 percent).

The excess supply of money causes individuals to turn to the assets market in an attempt to get rid of excess money balances.

71

This causes asset prices to rise more rapidly than before. Because the rise in asset prices at this higher rate is initially unexpected, the impact is a fall in nominal interest rates (and real rates as well). It also causes the beginning of gradual increases in supply for both bonds and equities. By the end of the process, the supply of bonds will have caught up with demand increases and bond prices and interest rates will return to their initial levels which are consistent with a 7 and not a 9 percent rate of increase in the money supply. This, however, does assume that the 9 percent rise is a temporary once-and-for-all deviation from the 7 percent trend. What happens when the 9 percent rate becomes the trend instead of the exception will be covered in the next section. Thus, interest rates temporarily fall and then begin slowly rising again.

The same thing happens in the equities market. The prices of equities initially rise faster than 7 percent and rates of return fall because resource returns are still rising at 7 percent. There is some initial increase in resource production, but this will be wiped out by overutilization of resources later in the process. The main reason that equity rates of return will eventually return to initial levels consistent with the 7 percent rate of rise in the money supply is that returns will eventually also begin to reflect the inflation override by catching up with asset prices.

In the goods market, the effect of lower rates of return in the asset markets will be to stimulate both consumption and investment demands. Prices will begin rising at greater than the expected 3 percent rate and profit margins will temporarily increase. Firms will try to increase output to take advantage of this situation as long as override price rises are still greater than rises in costs of production. This will create a business "boom" of rising real output that will last until costs of production have caught up with prices.

As before, the resource services market will be the last to be affected. As prices rise in the goods market and firm profit margins rise, firms will begin to demand more resource services to produce more output. Real resource returns will actually have fallen at this point because price rises have been more rapid than wage and rent increases. Thus, firms resort to the overtime tactic to acquire more labor and higher maintenance costs to acquire more resource services. Firms bidding for more resources gradually cause wages and rents to catch up with prices, at which time profit margins return to normal, as does the supply of resource services.

For a time thereafter, resource input levels are likely to drop below initial levels on a per unit basis. This may be hard to detect in a growth situation because some number of new resources are steadily entering the market, but there will be a time of recovery for older resources. Workers will take longer vacations and more sick leave, while machines will have more down time for postponed repairs. After this effect is gradually eliminated, a normal growth pattern is restored at the 7 percent money supply growth level, with 4 percent real growth and 3 percent inflation.

The Formation of Expectations

In the previous discussion, it was specified that the outcomes being discussed depended on the assumption of a once-and-for-all 2 percent deviation from the 7 percent long run rate of increase in the money supply. If, in fact, the shift to a 9 percent rate was more permanent, other affects would begin to be felt. It would take about six months after the initial increase in the rate of monetary expansion began for changes to show up prominently in the price level. After this, for another six months or more, the general expectation would be that this was a short term deviation from trend. The expected rate of inflation would continue for at least this period of time at 3 percent even though the actual rate would be approaching 5 percent. However, as time went on and the 5 percent rate continued, the economy would enter a period of inflationary uncertainty, with special effects to be described shortly.

During this period of uncertainty, individuals would gradually become aware that the 5 percent rate of inflation was continuing. There would be uncertainty because individuals would not be sure whether the actual rate of inflation would eventually return to

73

3 percent, remain at 5 percent or settle at some point between 3 and 5 percent. This uncertainty might last several years, but *if* the rate of inflation remained consistently at 5 percent, the expected rate of inflation would eventually arrive at this level.

When it did, the economy would settle into a full adjustment pattern around the expectation that the 5 percent inflation would continue indefinitely. The inflation override in interest rates and in expected appreciation on real assets would become 5 percent. Wages and rents would also be rising at an expected and real rate of 5 percent and so forth.

The Effects on Price Level Uncertainty

There remains one extremely important expectation factor— one that plays a regular role in day to day modern situations. This is the problem of uncertainty about future price levels. Inflationary uncertainty exists when individuals are unsure what the rate of change in the price level will be. This is quite different from a situation in which individuals and firms have a reasonable degree of confidence that the rate will be zero or 3 percent or 5 percent or any other rate. This is a situation in which some amount of inflation (or deflation) may be expected, but the exact amount is unclear to most investors, lenders and borrowers.

In such a situation, the expected rate of inflation is not a completely open question. The problem is rather that, within some range, the expected rate of inflation is uncertain. The best way to view this is to treat the expected rate of inflation as the center of the range within which the amount of inflation (or deflation) is expected to fall. Uncertainty can then be defined as the number of percentage points on either side of that center rate individuals feel define the range within which the outcome will fall. In this sense, if individuals expect the rate of inflation to fall between 3 and 5 percent, 4 percent is the expected rate of inflation with a 1 percent degree of uncertainty. The 1 percent of uncertainty reflects the fact that individuals expect the rate of inflation to fall within one percent of the expected 4 percent rate.

74

In the real world, no matter how stable the price level has been, there will always be some degree of uncertainty. But that degree can be greater or smaller and, of course, its impact depends on its magnitude. That impact is one of changing the nature of individual and firm planning. Any stable rate can be adjusted to, whether it is inflationary, deflationary or constant. Uncertainty can be adjusted for, but not adjusted to. Speculators can take out some of the effects of uncertainty by betting on their abilities to predict outcomes, but some kinds of plans cannot be covered by speculators—for example, whether or not to purchase new resources. Clearly, uncertainty will generate more conservatism in firm purchases of resources.

It also shifts the relative attractiveness of assets in favor of equities and away from bonds. This is because bond values at maturity are fixed in nominal terms, while equity values are free to adjust for inflation. When inflationary uncertainty is small, bonds are less risky investments than real assets. But with inflationary uncertainty, this relative advantage of bonds disappears and may even reverse itself. This, in turn, has the effect of causing bond prices to fall relative to real assets.

This is the truth behind the widely circulated notion that stocks are relatively "inflation proof" in comparison with bonds. The issue is *not* the amount of inflation itself, but rather the degree of uncertainty around that rate. When inflation is fully anticipated, stocks and bonds are equally "inflation proof" in the sense that their rates of return (when stock appreciation is counted as a "return") have inflation premiums to cover loss of purchasing power. It is only when inflation is uncertain that stocks become more responsive to actual changes in the price level than bonds. This is extremely important because inflationary uncertainty is a common phenomenon in all modern economies.

International Complications

The final explicit assumption to be relaxed is a minor one in comparison with the no-growth and no-price level expectation assumptions. This is the assumption of an absence of complications from the international economy. In the American economy where exports and imports are approximately 5 percent of national output, only very large changes in the international economy would have important effects on the domestic economy if it were not for the actions of government officials. However, the international economy does have some effect and that effect is significantly exaggerated by the overemphasis placed on it by government officials. There are times when monetary authorities have been far more concerned about the 5 percent of the economy that is involved in international transactions than the remaining 95 percent.

Here, several considerations must be noted that slightly modify earlier conclusions. For the most part, these lie in noting that international demands on the American economy are premised on somewhat different factors than internal demands. For example, internal low interest rates may cause American lenders to lend abroad. If so, the proportionality of changes in the bonds market to changes in the money market may be violated with the effect that bond prices may not rise as high as they would in the absence of an international effect.

Likewise, given fixed exchange rates in international money markets, inflation will cause an outflow of money into foreign countries and a reduction in foreign demands for domestic goods and services. Foreign demands will fall because inflation means that it will require more foreign currency to buy any given amount of domestic goods and services—unless, of course, foreign inflation is just as rapid (or more rapid with the opposite effect) as domestic inflation. For example, if the French franc trades at a rate of 5 francs to the dollar and the dollar inflates by 10 percent, it will cost $5\frac{1}{2}$ francs to buy the $1.10 necessary to purchase what 5 francs would purchase previously. Falling foreign demands would, of course, offset some of the additional inflation that would otherwise be expected.

These effects must be accounted for in preparing economic forecasts, but they do not change fundamental conclusions reached earlier.

Conclusion

This then ends the discussion of the effects of expanding the monetary supply for the time being. There does remain one more important issue inherent in the mechanisms that are used in practice to expand the money supply. It will, however, be useful to postpone this until after the discussion of the policy controls of the Federal Reserve System in Chapter 6. Then, in Chapter 7, the entire process will be reduced to more of a timing formula for investment purposes. For the moment, the discussion turns to the opposite side of the money supply situation—the effects of contracting the money supply (or increasing it slower than expected).

Chapter Five

When Money is Subtracted

In this chapter, the focus centers on the effects of contracting the money supply. In most respects, the effects of contracting the money supply are just opposite those of expanding the money supply. There are, however, a few differences that are important. Further, there are enough things going on in response to monetary changes that it is likely that the readers of the previous chapter will not be unhappy to see a recap of the same material aimed at the opposite effects.

Following the same format as in the previous chapter, this one will begin with the same initial assumptions as the previous one: (1) no real economic growth; (2) no expectations of changes in the price level; (3) no international complications; and (4) that in the period prior to introduced changes in the money supply was one of full economic adjustments in all markets. And, again, the decline in the money supply will not be explained, pending the discussion of the monetary system in Chapter 6.

Into this situation, a reduction in the money supply will be introduced. And, as before, the first discussion will be an overview of the adjustment process that concentrates on price level and real output effects.

Price Level Effects

In the money market, the initial impact of a reduction in the money supply is that the supply of money will not be large enough to meet the existing demand. Individuals and firms will find themselves short of cash balances. To rectify this situation, both individuals and firms begin to attempt to increase cash balances. They attempt to do this initially in the bonds market, but shortly also turn to the equities market. In both cases, however, it is important to remember that the money market adjusts through a change in demand and that the now smaller money supply remains constant throughout the process.

The attempt to get more money by selling bonds reduces the general demand for bonds. This causes interest rates to rise. Again, if a bond costing $200 and yielding $10 in interest has its price fall from $200 to $180, the interest rate will rise from 5 to 5.55 percent. Ten dollars in interest is 5 percent of $200, but 5.55 percent of $180. This rise in interest rates will mean that bonds have temporarily better yields than equities. This is obvious since the two rates started at equal levels (when risk differences are accounted for) and interest rates rose while the rate of returns on equities remained briefly at initial levels.

At this point, it becomes more attractive to sell equities to acquire desired cash balances. The demand for real assets consequently falls, lagging only slightly behind the fall in the demand for bonds. The reduction in demand causes equity prices to fall with both the effect that the demand for new producer goods falls and that rates of return on equities rise. (The returns, as

80

distinct from the rate of returns, have not yet changed while asset prices have fallen.)

In the goods market, the rise in yields on both bonds and equities causes individuals to defer consumption expenditures to the future. And, at the same, carrying over from the equities market, the demand for investment goods has also fallen. This creates a downward pressure on the price level that continues until full adjustment is restored in the money market.

Real Output Effects

It is at this point that the contraction effects diverge from a perfect symmetry with expansion effects. The reduction in demand in the goods market causes a reduction in output supplies in addition to its price level effects, but there is no inverse parallel to the overtime pricing tactic in an expansion process. What happens instead is unemployment.

As the demand for goods and services declines, firms find their profit margins pinched and try to reduce output. In doing so, they reduce their demands for resources services, laying off workers, and cancelling orders for new equipment, letting machines sit idle to avoid maintenance costs and so forth. In the resource services market, this means that the quantity effect of a change in demand is initially much stronger than the price effect. This brings up the issue of downward wage rigidities mentioned in Chapter 2. There are reasons for this effect. Union pressure operates against wage reductions and long term rental contracts operate against real reductions. Those resources a firm owns may not see declines in rents, but they may be allowed to sit idle to avoid maintenance repair costs. The overall impact is a recessionary economy.

Downward rigidities are not, however, permanent obstacles to adjustment in the resource services market. Downward adjustments in wages and rents begin immediately but may take a number of months to proceed—depending on severity, as long as 15 months.

81

Workers may, in fact, prefer to remain on unemployment compensation rather than accept a lower wage as long as they continue to draw unemployment checks. But when the period of compensation runs out, they are forced to seek new employment, even at lower wages. As wages and rents gradually adjust downward, the quantity demanded increases and unemployment gradually disappears. Output, of course, falls and then returns to normal as this is going on.

At this point, there is a tendency for resource inputs to temporarily increase beyond initial levels. This secondary reaction parallels the temporary recuperation period in the expansion process. As an economy emerges from a recession, workers are still suffering from previous losses in real income and are certainly more than well rested. They will tend to offer more hours of labor than they will continue to offer in the long run. They will do this both because of a desire to make up part of their lost incomes and because long hours of labor seem less onerous after imposed rest through unemployment.

This temporarily available larger supply of resource services will cause real output to increase temporarily above its long-run full adjustment path. This jump in output will level back toward its initial size as normal patterns of employment gradually reassert themselves. On this basis, it is useful to note that an economy somewhat compensates for output gains during booms and output losses during recessions.

As in the previous chapter, specific effects in specific markets will now be outlined, beginning with the money market.

The Money Market

In the money market, the first stage of the adjustment process begins with the decline in the supply of money. Since nothing has operated to change the demand for money at this point, demand now exceeds supply. As individuals attempt to turn to other markets in order to replace lost money balances, there is a sense in which they must fail. The supply of money is now smaller and, in aggregate, this fact cannot be changed. But individuals will succeed in approaching full adjustment in the sense that their attempts to acquire more money will cause changes that will, in turn, reduce their demands for money to the point that it will eventually equal the smaller money supply.

As in the case of the expansion process, there will be three different factors that will operate to reduce the demand for money, but only one of these will be permanent. And, although only one is permanent, the temporary impact of the other two will be such that the money market will approach a state of full adjustment somewhat faster than other markets. This will be seen as the attempt to acquire more money causes individuals to turn first to the bonds market, then to real assets and finally to the market for goods and services.

The attempt to acquire money by selling assets, as has been seen, leads to lower asset prices and both a higher interest rate and a higher rate of return on equities. The rise in these two rates are the temporary factors in the restoration of full adjustment in the money market. By the end of the total adjustment process, they will return to approximately their initial levels. But while they are temporarily higher, they have the effect of reducing the demand for money. As discussed in Chapter 3, the interest rate and the rate of return on equities are both opportunity costs of holding money. When they rise, then, the demand for money will fall. Thus, during the part of the process that these rates are temporarily higher, they will have a downward effect on the demand for money.

Even at the early stages of the adjustment process, the money demand effects of lower asset yields are supported by a beginning fall in the price level in the goods market. The price level is another factor in the demand for money and its fall will also cause the demand for money to decline. Thus, in the early stages of the general adjustment process following a decline in the money supply, there are three different reasons for a declining demand for money—a rising interest rate, a rising rate of return on equities and a declining price level.

As the process of adjustment continues, however, effects in other markets will begin to reverse the initial rises in asset rates of return. A declining supply of bonds will gradually cause interest rates to fall back toward initial levels. Likewise, forces will act to reverse the initial rise in rates of return on equities and they also will return toward initial levels. As this happens, only the continuing downward movement of the price level sustains itself to reduce the demand for money to the level of the money supply.

In the end, the money market will show a decline in demand proportionate to the money supply and the technical price of money, the inverse of the price level, will be higher. This is because, with a lower price level, the purchasing power of each dollar would be lower. Hence, the number of goods and services that must be given up in order to hold a dollar as cash balances is smaller.

The Bonds Market

The first place individuals turn when they are short of money is the bonds market. They attempt to sell bonds or borrow money (both of which have the same effect) in order to restore cash balances to desired levels. In a practical sense they cannot succeed because there simply is not enough money to meet the existing demand, but they can and do reduce their demands for bonds. This causes the price of bonds to fall and bond interest rates to correspondingly rise. This is the most pronounced effect in the early part of the adjustment process.

As interest rates rise, however, it becomes more expensive for both firms and individuals to borrow. As the interest individuals and firms must pay to borrow or give up by not saving is higher, the rate of borrowing begins to decline, gradually reducing the total number of bonds available in the economy. This gradual

84

reduction in supply will slowly reverse the direction of bond prices. They will begin to return to initial levels. When they have, interest rates will have correspondingly fallen back to approximately their initial levels.

In the end, though the nominal prices have fallen and then returned to initial levels, the *real* value of each remaining bond will be permanently higher. Those who have held bonds throughout the adjustment process are better off than before the decline in the money supply. This is because the money they will be paid back will purchase more goods and services than the money they lent. From society's standpoint, however, the total *stock* of bonds will have the same real value as before the decline in money. The *nominal* amount of bonds will be smaller than before because of the reduction in the number of bonds issued, but the number of bonds will have decreased in approximate proportion to the gain in value of the bonds that remain. For example, if the overall fall in the price level was 2 percent, each bond will be worth 2 percent more in real terms than before the decline in the money supply. If, at the same time, the number of bonds has declined by 2 percent, the total real value of bonds will equal the original real value of the initially larger number of bonds.

Equities

As in the case of bonds, the initial impact of a decline in the money supply on the equities market is a reduction in the demand for equities. This will cause equity prices to fall. This effect will lag slightly, but only slightly, behind the fall in bond prices and is caused by the same supply and demand forces involved in the fall in bond prices. When equity prices fall, their returns will not yet have been affected. Thus, their rates of return will necessarily rise.

The reduced demand for equities will also affect the quantity supplied of equities in the sense that the demand for new producer goods will have fallen. This means that new producer good prices will fall and firms producing them will reduce output. This reduction in producer good output is small and will probably be cancelled out later in the adjustment process by the temporary real output spurt at its end.

The reason that the reduced output of producer goods is a short-lived phenomenon is that the returns on equities soon begin to fall as wages and rents begin to fall in proportion to the initial fall in equity prices. As this happens, costs of production in producer good industries decline and their output levels return to normal. These returns continue to fall until the original rate of return is restored. Thus, at the end of the adjustment process, equity prices—unlike bond prices—will be permanently lower, but with rates of return equal to initial levels. Investors who held equities through the entire adjustment process will tend to have neither gained nor lost purchasing power at its end.

From the standpoint of society, it is possible that the total stock of resources will have fallen. This, however, must be seen in the context of the fact that the recession portion of the adjustment process will cause resources not being used to last longer. There may or may not be any long run net loss of resources.

The Goods Market

In the goods market, the first effect derives from a decrease in both consumer and investment demands. The decrease in consumer demand is caused by the temporarily higher interest rates and rates of return on equities. With a higher reward for saving and opportunity cost of consumption, there is greater incentive for individuals to postpone consumption until the future. Likewise, when loans are more costly, individuals are less likely to borrow to increase their holdings of real assets. Thus, both the consumption and investment demands for goods and services decline in response to higher interest rates.

This reduction in demand causes the prices of goods and services (and hence the price level) to fall. Falling prices at a time when costs of production are still stable cause profit margins to decline. Firms begin to cut back on production. Real output declines and the economy enters a recessionary phase. As this happens, firms release resources from employment and a general condition of unemployment develops. This further accelerates the drop in the demand for goods and services because the incomes of resource owners decline and they demand fewer goods and services.

However, as unemployment develops, resources are in excess supply and wages and rents begin to fall. This gradual decline in wages and rents means that costs of production of firms also decline. And, in turn, as costs of production fall, firm profit margins begin to restore themselves. Gradually, since resource prices are falling, firms begin rehiring resources and output levels begin to move back toward initial levels. Full employment begins to be reestablished.

At this point, the economy will tend to enjoy a small output spurt over normal full employment levels. Plant and equipment will tend to be in better than average condition after the layoff and will be used more intensively until normal repair patterns reassert themselves. Likewise, workers will be well rested after periods of unemployment and leave time and absenteeism will tend to be lower than normal as workers look for ways to make up part of the incomes they lost during the recession.

After this temporary spurt, the economy returns to its normal production patterns with both prices and costs of production proportionally reduced. Money profits will be lower in nominal terms than before the decline in the money supply, but the *rate* of profit will be the same as it was initially. *Real* profits will be no lower than before, both in terms of dollars and as a rate.

The Resource Service Market

The resource service market is affected as the demand for goods and services declines. The resource services market is thus the last market to be affected. It is something of an anomaly, but resource owners have benefited from the initial effects of the decline in the money supply just before they begin to find their resources unemployed. Since, at this point, prices have fallen, but wages and rents are still at their initial levels, the real purchasing power of those wages and rents will have risen. Workers and machines will thus be earning higher real wages and real rents.

This effect, however, is short-lived. Almost immediately, workers begin being laid off and machines begin to sit idle as profit-starved firms begin to reduce output levels. Firms, in effect, cannot afford to pay the same wages and rents they could afford when the prices at which they can sell output was higher. The economy enters its recessionary stage. The unemployment of resources is, in economic terms, an excess supply of resource services. It is an excess supply that will have the normal market effect of forcing prices down, in this case wages and rents. But the market for resource services is subject to downward rigidities. Union pressure, the existence of long-term rental contracts and firm direct ownership of resources all act as barriers that slow up the downward price effects. There are also other institutional problems to complement these.

This, however, does not mean an indefinite period of unemployment, as Keynes appeared to think. It is in reference to this part of the adjustment process that Keynes was asked whether wages would not fall in the long run. He replied, "Yes, but in the long run we are all dead." The long run is not that long. It is a matter of months and not lifetimes. The downward adjustment process may be tortuous and slow, but it is resolute. Wages and rents do fall and, as they do, firm profit margins gradually restore themselves. And, as profits return to normal, so does the real demand for resource services. This gradual returning to normal of the demand for resource services can also be seen in a more direct way. As resource service prices fall, the demand for them will naturally increase. Eventually, both employment and output return to normal at lower nominal wages and rents that have the same real purchasing power as before the monetary disturbance.

This, again, will be followed by a period during which resource service offerings—both human and nonhuman—will temporarily exceed normal levels. Workers will be rested and willing to work longer hours to make up some of the earlier income losses. Machines will tend to be in good repair and unneedful of normal repair maintenance for a period of time. As normal patterns reassert themselves, the economy will return to its long run trend.

Adjustment with Growth

Having completed this discussion of the effects of a decline of the money supply in the simplest possible circumstances, the initial assumptions of the model will be progressively relaxed. This parallels perfectly the format of the previous chapter. The assumptions on which the previous discussion was based were: (1) no real economic growth; (2) no expectations of changes in the price level; (3) no international complications; and (4) that the process began with a condition of full adjustment in all markets. These will be relaxed in turn. One difference in this chapter as compared to the last will be that the final assumption of initial full adjustment will be specifically considered.

As was discussed in the previous chapter, a condition of a long-run trend in real economic growth is normal and implies a different conception of full economic adjustment than was used in the very simple model. Growth means that the supply of goods and services is increasing over time. A long-run trend in growth means that the rate of increase is relatively consistent from year to year, but allows for some deviation up and down. When growth meets the trend condition, as it normally does, its consequences can be planned for in all parts of the economy in a way that produces a full adjustment mechanism.

This growth oriented full adjustment mechanism is dynamic in character, with supplies and demands in all markets (except the *nominal* supply of money) increasing in similar growth patterns. As growth occurs, it is obvious that society is gradually increasing its stock of productive resources. This means that the underlying

"realness" of equities is increasing. Since much of these new resources and some of the increase in consumption is being financed
by increased borrowing, the supply of bonds is increasing. Firms
trying to increase output are demanding more resource services
and incomes are rising. With larger incomes, individuals demand
more goods and services, bonds, real assets, and money. Only the
supply of money is free of the dynamics of this growth process,
and it only because of the nature of governmental control of the
monetary system.

In the previous chapter, it was shown that unless decisions
were made to increase the supply of money as fast as or slightly
faster than the supply of goods and services, the price level would
fall. That, of course, remains true here and does not require
repetition. The way to maintain a constant price level is to increase
the supply of money at a rate similar to the rate of real economic
growth.

The Role of Expectations

When individuals expect changes in the price level to be occurring over time, the meaning of a decline in the money supply
must be modified to a *relative* decline. This again parallels the
expansion process except that it has much more relevance to the
real world. On the expansion side, if the money supply declined,
but declined at a rate lower than would justify expectations of a
falling price level, the economy could enter a *deflationary boom*.
That does not happen in today's world. But if the money supply
does not increase fast enough to justify inflationary expectations,
the economy enters a stage of *inflationary recession*. That does
happen and far too frequently.

It is important in a world of normal inflation to think of a
relative decline in the money supply instead of absolute declines.
For present purposes, "relative" means relative to the rate that
would permit expectations to be realized. Thus, for example, if
the growth rate was 4 percent, the expected rate of inflation was

90

5 percent and the money supply had been growing at 9 percent per year, any rate of increases less than 9 percent would be an example of a relative decline in the money supply.

A relative decline in the money supply in this sense will cause recessionary effects that will closely parallel the actual reduction of money units in the initial model of this chapter. In going through this, it is crucial to remember that price level effects of monetary changes are not immediate and must await partial completion of the adjustment process. And, as in the previous chapter, it will be assumed initially that although some amount of inflation is expected, it is a relatively certain amount so that the effects of inflationary uncertainty are not important. This special assumption will be relaxed shortly.

With a real growth rate of 4 percent and an expected rate of inflation of 5 percent, the existing condition in the money market would be one of both demand for and supply of money increasing at a rate of or slightly more than 9 percent. A relative decline in the money supply would mean any rate of increase less than 9 percent, here 7 percent for exposition in specific terms. A 7 percent increase in the money supply would be 2 percent less than the amount necessary to justify price level expectations.

Under these circumstances, an excess demand for money develops in the money market and individuals begin to try to accumulate more cash balances by selling of (or not buying as many) other assets—first bonds and then equities. Thus the demands for assets begin to increase at lower rates than the supplies are increasing. Excess supplies are created in the bonds and equities markets. Prices of these assets begin to fall (or rise at slower rates) and the interest rate and rates of return on equities begin to rise.

As asset rates of return rise, the costs of consumption and investment borrowing rise. Consumption and investment demands for goods and services rise less rapidly and an excess supply of goods develops. Prices continue to rise, but more slowly than before. Further, firms attempt to reduce output and begin laying off workers and letting machines sit idle. The economy enters a recessionary phase even though inflation is continuing (at a somewhat slower rate).

The attempt by firms to reduce output creates a decline in the demand for resource services. This is manifested by an excess supply of resource services—the unemployment condition. Unemployment causes wages and rents to begin increasing less rapidly than previously. Slowly, but surely, wages and rents return to their initial proportionality to the price level, thereby reducing relative costs of production. As this happens, the economy slowly returns to full employment and temporarily spurts ahead of its long run real output trend as rested formerly unemployed resources are used somewhat more intensively. All other markets slowly return to normal in the manner described previously.

The Effects of Deflationary Uncertainty

The effects of inflationary uncertainty arise whenever inflation is expected, but the amount is uncertain. The effect that such a circumstance makes equities relatively more attractive than bonds was discussed in the previous chapter and does not need to be repeated here. It does not matter whether the uncertainty arises from a potential decline in the rate of inflation rather than a potential rise, as in the previous chapter. The expected rate of inflation continues to be defined as the center of the range in which inflation might be expected to fall. Given uncertainty about the rate of inflation, stocks become somewhat safer and bonds more risky—relative to each other—than when the expected rate of inflation is regarded as more certain.

Here, and only for logical completeness, the possibility of deflationary uncertainty in the relative attractiveness of bonds versus real assets will be considered. At the present time, the practical relevance of such a situation seems remote, but the real world has a way of changing in unexpected ways. In any case, this situation did arise in the latter part of the nineteenth century and it may be an interesting historical footnote.

If, in fact, individuals expect some given rate of deflation, but are uncertain as to the amount, it is again true that bond prices are less responsive to deviations from the expected rate than real asset prices. Thus, as in the case of inflationary uncertainty, deflationary uncertainty increases the riskiness of bonds relative to real assets. This increases the relative demand for real assets and reduces the relative demand for bonds as methods of storing purchasing power for the future. Stock prices will be somewhat higher and bond prices somewhat lower on a relative basis when this occurs.

International Complications

International complications must be considered, but they are not different in this chapter from the last.

Changes When Adjustment Is Not Complete

In the real world, monetary changes seldom fit simple patterns of changes that allow full adjustment to one pattern to be completed before the next pattern begins. For this reason, none of the versions of the adjustment mechanisms outlined in the past two chapters ever operates in the perfect situations assumed for purposes of explanation. The Federal Reserve Board, in ways that will be described in the next chapter, frequently causes the money supply to expand drastically in one month and then turns around and holds it constant or even contracts it in the next.

Obviously, when this happens, the adjustment process reacting to what happened in the expansionary month is not completed when the second month's effects begin. The expansionary month's effects are just getting started. Just as obvious is the fact that it is very difficult to pin down what effects derive from what month's worth of changes in the money supply. This problem is further complicated by the fact that the timing of various effects is not always identical. The various stages of the adjustment process from any one change may occur sooner or later than similar changes under slightly different circumstances. There may be a dozen sets of effects operating at once, each one of which has the effects described in the past two chapters. But the effects from some of the adjustments may cancel out others so that the real world outcomes are very confused, especially to the observer who does not know what to look for.

What to look for is the subject of Chapter 7. Before that, it will be useful to look at how and why monetary changes take place.

Chapter Six

The Money Makers

In most modern economies (other than in the communist bloc), the control of money rests with some sort of central bank. In different societies, the central bank may have greater or lesser degrees of autonomy from the rest of government. Regardless of where the authority to make decisions for a central bank finally rests, its power is tremendous. The power to make money is the power to stabilize or destroy an economy. Governments have risen and fallen on the power of money makers. This chapter deals with how that power is exercised in the United States.

In Great Britain, the central bank is the Bank of England. There is a Bank of Canada, a Bank of France, a Bank of Belgium and of many other free world countries. There is no Bank of the United States, largely because of political quarrels between Andrew Jackson and Nicholas Biddle, president of the Second

Bank of the United States in the 1830s. Those quarrels are not the subject of the present work. Instead, the focus here is on the American institution that substitutes for a central bank—the Federal Reserve System.

On paper, the Federal Reserve System is a system of twelve regional central banks guided by a board of governors for the entire system. In practice, although there is some regional autonomy in the individual banks, the system does not differ much from a true central bank of the types found in other economies of the free world. The important decisions are made by committees responsible to the Federal Reserve Board and not by the presidents or policy mechanisms of the individual banks spread over the country. Reams of material could be written about the institutional arrangements of the Federal Reserve System (henceforth Fed), but the concern here is only with the mechanisms used in the creation of money.

Technically, there are two basic kinds of ways that money can be created. One is the production of *fiat* money. This is done by cranking up the printing presses and printing new money that is then spent by the Treasury (or whoever else happens to get hold of it). Fiat money is simply money by law because the government specifies that it must be accepted in payment within the society the government controls. Implicitly, earlier discussions of changes in the money supply were based on this type of money creation in spite of the fact that it is relatively unusual in the context of the American economy. U. S. Notes, which can still occasionally be found in circulating currency (including all $2 bills, for example) are fiat money in this sense. Silver certificates were technically not fiat money, but in fact were very similar in practice.

The reasons earlier discussions were based on this relatively unusual form of money creation instead of the more common type of creation through the banking system (to be discussed below) are two: first, the process of adjustment is somewhat simpler with fiat money; second, it is useful to consider the effects of money creation before considering how money creation occurs. The banking system type of creation raises issues it is hard to understand without first understanding the banking system. The use of the fiat money mechanism avoids these problems.

This chapter, then, has three objectives. First, it will explain the process of money creation in the present American banking system. Second, it will explain the mechanisms the Fed has to control that process. And third, 'it will explain how this type of money creation modifies earlier discussions of the effects of changing the money supply.

The Role of Reserve Requirements

Both of the definitions of money emphasized earlier, M_1 and M_2, include bank deposits as a form of money. M_1 includes currency in circulation plus demand deposits in checking accounts. M_2 includes currency in circulation plus both demand and time deposits—but only in banks. Time deposit equivalents in other kinds of savings institutions are not included. The reasons for this latter fact will become more evident as the process of money creation through banks is considered.

There are two ways that bank deposits are generated. One occurs when individuals make deposits from income or firms make deposits from revenue received. In such transactions, the bank receives assets in the form of money or claims on other banks and a liability in the form of the depositor's right to reclaim the amount of the deposit. The second form may occur when individuals borrow money from banks. When individuals borrow, they sign notes promising to repay money in the future and receive present money that is frequently handled as credits to their checking accounts. In such cases, the bank receives a note as an asset and acquires the demand deposit as a liability. Both types of demand deposit creation are involved in bank creation of new money.

To see how, one must first look at the function of bank reserve requirement ratios. Banks must keep currency on reserve against their outstanding deposits. This may be held either in bank

97

vaults or in deposits with the Fed. Bank deposits are claims against the bank for money that can be exercised at any time by depositors. This is a legal requirement of demand deposits. With time deposits, banks are legally prohibited from promising to pay in less than 30 days, but in practice time deposits are also paid on demand. This means that the bank must have on hand, or in reserve with the Fed accounts, enough cash to meet the daily demands of their depositors.

But it does not mean that they must have on hand enough cash to satisfy *all* of their depositors. All of their depositors are not going to demand all of their deposits on any one day. It is therefore unnecessary for a bank to keep on hand enough cash reserves to pay off all their deposits. What they do hold is some fraction of total deposits in reserve. Before the institution of the Federal Reserve System in 1914, banks selected this fraction on the basis of business judgment and practice. After 1914, this fraction has been regulated by the Fed, with policy results that will be considered later.

The method of regulation has been the specification of a required minimum percentage (or fraction) of total deposits that banks must hold. This percentage is called a *required reserve rate*. It has varied somewhat over time and is slightly higher for "city" banks than "country" banks, but has generally stayed in the range of 20 percent for demand deposits and between 5 and 10 percent for time deposits. Recently, rates have been based on a complicated formula based on bank size and location. In some ways these rates reflect what was regarded as conservative, or "safe," bank practice prior to 1914.

The reason for setting reserve requirements was a recurrent problem of bank "runs" in the nineteenth century. Bank runs occur when depositors try to reclaim their deposits within a very short period of time. Banks that maintained low reserve fractions were more vulnerable to this problem than banks with higher reserve fractions. Bank "runs" were created by a temporary loss of confidence in given banks, although they could easily become general and create a *panic* situation for the entire banking system.

Such losses of confidence were sometimes based on legitimate concerns of bank depositors, but all too often they were a consequence of idle rumor.

In either case, the loss of confidence would feed on itself as rumors ran wild through a community. Depositors, who were then unprotected by Federal Deposit Insurance Corporation guarantees, would line up at the bank or banks in question, hoping to recover their deposits before bank reserves ran out. Sometimes, as a bank continued to pay out cash to depositors, confidence was somehow restored, in which case lines of waiting depositors dissipated and the crisis ended. But when bank reserves ran out before confidence could be restored, the bank that could not borrow from other banks would be forced into bankruptcy, or into suspending the convertibility of deposits into currency. As this happened, depositors who had not gotten their money out in time could lose all or most of their deposits. The Federal Reserve Act of 1914 was designed to prevent precisely this problem, although it failed miserably from 1929–1933—a failure that caused the Great Depression.

The establishment of minimum reserve requirements has caused banks to become even more conservative than might be apparent in the required reserve rates themselves. Since the reserve requirements set a legal minimum reserve requirement, a bank that stayed close to the requirement would be constantly in danger that a slight shift in depositors' behavior could throw their reserve holdings below the required level. To avoid this, banks actually maintain a margin of safety above the required minimum. This extra margin of safety will vary between banks, but an assumption of 5 percent will be used here. For this reason, 25 percent will be taken as a working measure of reserve holdings of banks for a discussion of the money creation process. Of that 5 percent is the bank's desired margin of safety above the reserve requirement of 20 percent.

The same kind of logic holds for time deposits. The time deposit reserve rate is lower because time depositors reclaim their deposits less frequently than demand depositors. Thus, it is safe for banks to hold lower reserves against them. This is also reflected in laws setting lower minimum requirements against time deposits than demand deposits. Time deposit reserve rate requirements have varied between 3 and 10 percent. An 8 percent figure will be taken as a working average. Banks again wish to avoid trying to operate at exactly the legal minimum and maintain a margin of safety. Because of the greater stability of time deposits, the margin of safety can be smaller than the 5 percent on demand deposits. Here, 2 percent can serve as an adequate figure. Thus, for discussion of the money creation process, a 10 percent measure of fractional bank reserve holdings against time deposits will be employed.

The stage is now set for the money creation process.

The Process of Bank Money Creation

In this discussion, it will be assumed that before the change in bank reserves that will be introduced, every bank in the banking system is in a position such that it is holding its desired 25 percent reserves against its outstanding demand deposits and 10 percent against its outstanding time deposits. For example, if a bank had $10 million in demand deposits and $7 million in time deposits, it would need to hold a total of $3.2 million in cash reserves—$2.5 million to back its demand deposits and $.7 million to back its time deposits. Such a bank is said to be "fully lent up."

If each bank is in the same position, banks will not be in a position to expand their demand deposits unless they somehow acquire more cash reserves. The banking system always tends to move toward such a situation because reserves in excess of what are needed are not earning interest banks could earn if they increased loans. Banks therefore tend to extend loans out to the point that their desired limit is reached. Only if more reserves are somehow brought into the system would the volume of loans expand and with them, for reasons below, the total stock of deposits.

100

Those new reserves would result from individuals deciding to increase their deposits of currency in banks. This, however, is very unlikely in practice because the currency to deposit ratio is generally stable and not subject to random changes of the sort that would be required. A much more likely type of change would involve the purchase of bank holdings of government bonds by the Federal Reserve System. Such transactions are a part of Fed *open-market operations.*

The Fed, for example, might decide to purchase $1 million worth of U. S. Government bonds from commercial banks. The incentive for the banks to sell would be a price offering that was slightly above market. In this transaction, the Fed would give up currency in the form of Federal Reserve Notes and receive U. S. Government bonds. The currency given up by the Fed could either be from Fed vaults or from currency recently printed by the Treasury at the request of the Fed. In both cases, the Fed would acquire matching liabilities and assets worth $1 million.

Likewise, the banks that sold bonds to the Fed would gain and lose assets worth $1 million. In practice, because the transaction must be attractive to the banks for them to be willing to sell bonds, there is some slight gain to the banks. But, on paper, banks gain assets worth $1 million in the form of Federal Reserve Notes and lose assets worth $1 million in the form of U. S. Government bonds. Thus, in the transaction itself, nothing has happened to affect significantly the financial position of either Fed or commercial banks.

Something, however, has happened to the cash reserve position of the banks that sold the bonds. They have traded assets in the form of bonds that *could not* be used as reserves against their deposits, for assets in the form of Federal Reserve Notes that *can* be used as reserves. In consequence, these banks now have $1 million in cash reserves that they do not need to hold. They can lend these out. They have an incentive to do so to gain the interest involved in making loans.

At this point, it will be useful to organize the discussion of the money creation process in the form of Table 6-1. The banks that sell bonds to the Fed will be designated as Banks A. Banks A will lend out money to individuals and firms in the amount of $1 million. Temporarily, this may create demand deposits in Banks A of $1 million. At this level of transactions, individuals and firms supply promises to pay $1 million plus interest in the future and receive $1 million in present money that may take the temporary form of demand deposits. These deposits, however, are likely to be short-lived because borrowers seldom borrow to hold demand deposits. Instead, it is very likely that these loan created deposits will rapidly be spent, either for consumer goods, for producer goods, or some other asset form.

As the sellers of these items receive payment from the borrowers who borrowed from Banks A, they will make deposits in Banks B. Banks A, at this point, will lose both deposits and cash reserves equaling $1 million. They will now have the same number of deposits and cash reserves as before the Fed bond transaction. Banks A will have, in effect, traded U. S. Government notes for promissory notes of borrowers, each worth $1 million. No money has yet been created.

With Banks B, it is different. Banks B, as the banks that receive deposits from the sellers of items to the borrowers from Banks A, acquire deposits and cash reserves of $1 million. These deposits are more stable than loan created deposits. Banks B can expect these deposits to remain for at least some period of time. Here, however, the form of deposits is important. This will be handled by assuming first that they are entirely demand deposits, as presented in Table 6-1. Then later, the entire process will be repeated with the assumption that they are entirely time deposits in Table 6-2. Actually, they will be both, but the necessary modification for this will be simple once the more extreme possibilities are considered.

Since, by assumption, these deposits are demand deposits and, by prior assumption, banks desire to maintain 25 percent reserves against demand deposits, Banks B desire to hold $250,000 (25 percent) against their new $1 million in deposits. This, of course, can be done out of the new $1 million in cash they have acquired through presenting claims on Banks A. Banks B thus find themselves holding $1 million in cash, of which they wish to hold $250,000 in new reserves. They therefore have *excess* cash reserves in the amount of $750,000 (see Table 6-1).

Thus, Banks B can lend out $750,000 and have an incentive to do so to gain the interest involved. These loans follow the same pattern as loans made by Banks A. Borrowers from Banks B may temporarily create demand deposits until they make purchases, but the purpose of their borrowing is to make purchases and not to hold demand deposits. Thus, the $750,000 and any temporarily loan created demand deposits will quickly leave Banks B, on their way to Banks C.

Again, as the borrowers from Banks B make purchases worth $750,000, this amount will be received by sellers who make deposits in Banks C. Banks C could include some of the same banks in groups A or B, but can still be referred to as some of Banks C for the purposes of this discussion. Banks C receive the $750,-000 in claims on Banks B that are immediately exercised to produce $750,000 in cash reserves. Against the increase of $750,000 in new demand deposits, they will want to hold $187,500 in increased reserves. The remaining $562,500 they will lend out.

The process, after lending, purchasing and depositing, creates $562,500 in new demand deposits in Banks D. Banks D keep $140,625 of the $562,500 cash reserves they also receive and lend out $421,875, which then goes to Banks E and so forth. This process continues through additional stages until the amounts have become vanishingly small. Results are presented for bank groups A through H in Table 6-1.

Each addition to demand deposits (+DD) in Table 6-1 is new money that has been added to the economic system by the transactions involved. When the process reaches Banks H, a total of $3,466,065 in new money has been created. The process, of course, does not stop with Banks H, but goes on until the amounts involved at each stage become vanishing small. At that point, the amount of new demand deposits would theoretically be $4 million. This is the amount of demand deposits that can be supported by

103

Table 6-1

Money Expansion Process
(with Demand Deposits)

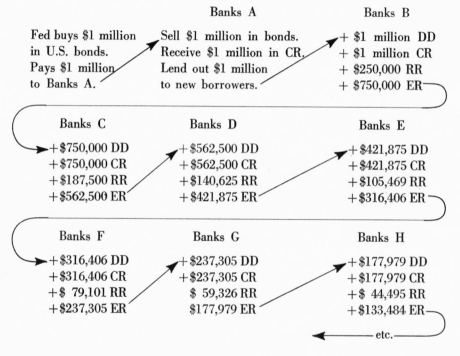

	Banks A	Banks B
Fed buys $1 million in U.S. bonds. Pays $1 million to Banks A.	Sell $1 million in bonds. Receive $1 million in CR. Lend out $1 million to new borrowers.	+ $1 million DD + $1 million CR + $250,000 RR + $750,000 ER

Banks C	Banks D	Banks E
+ $750,000 DD + $750,000 CR + $187,500 RR + $562,500 ER	+ $562,500 DD + $562,500 CR + $140,625 RR + $421,875 ER	+ $421,875 DD + $421,875 CR + $105,469 RR + $316,406 ER

Banks F	Banks G	Banks H
+ $316,406 DD + $316,406 CR + $ 79,101 RR + $237,305 ER	+ $237,305 DD + $237,305 CR $ 59,326 RR $177,979 ER	+ $177,979 DD + $177,979 CR + $ 44,495 RR + $133,484 ER

— etc. —

DD = Demand Deposits
CR = Cash Reserves (or equivalent Fed deposits)
RR = Dollar amount of required reserves
ER = Dollar amount of excess reserves

104

$1 million when banks maintain 25 percent reserves. One million dollars is 25 percent of $4 million. In practice, because some of the money would not be redeposited either through being kept as currency or by flowing to foreign countries, the actual expansion would be close to $2.5 million. The number 2.5 is the actual expansion factor for demand deposits alone in the American economy.

Expansion with Time Deposits

It will now be useful to consider what would have happened if after each set of transactions, the deposits had been time deposits instead of demand deposits. This is covered in Table 6-2. It is important to note that loan created deposits will *not* be assumed to be time deposits. These short-lived deposits would almost never take a time deposit form because of the lack of accessibility. But deposits following sales of goods and services or assets could well be deposited in time accounts, as is assumed here.

The process of expansion would begin again with purchases by the Fed of $1 million in U. S. Government bonds—the open market operation purchase. This would be a set of transactions involving the Fed and Banks A, who sold the bonds. Banks A would thus have $1 million in currency they did not require as reserves against outstanding deposits. To gain the interest involved, Banks A lend out this $1 million and cease to be part of the expansion process. On net, Banks A have exchanged $1 million in U. S. Government bonds for $1 million in personal notes.

The borrowers from Banks A make purchases and the beneficiaries make assumed time deposits in Banks B. Banks B have now acquired $1 million in time deposits liabilities and $1 million in currency claims on Banks A that are immediately exercised to provide actual currency. Of this currency, Banks B will want to hold 10 percent, or $100,000 against their time deposits. This leaves an excess of $900,000 that can be lent out. Again, there is an incentive to do so to gain the interest involved. It is also to be noted that this $900,000 that can be lent out is $150,000 larger than the $750,000 that could have been lent out if the deposit form had been demand deposits.

The borrowers from Banks B make purchases of $900,000 and the receivers of the $900,000 payments make time deposits in Banks C. Banks C thus receive $900,000 in time deposit liabilities and $900,000 in exercisable claims on Banks B for currency. Upon exercising these claims, Banks C retain $90,000 as a 10 percent reserve and lend out $810,000. This $810,000 is used for purchases and sellers deposit this amount in Banks D. Banks D have acquired $810,000 in new time deposit liabilities and $810,000 in exercisable currency claims on Banks C. Upon immediate exercise of these claims, Banks D retain $81,000 as reserves and lend out $729,000. Effects through Banks H are described in Table 6-2.

With the time deposit expansion process, the expansion factor is 10 rather than the factor of 4 found in time deposits. This is because of the differences in bank desired reserve ratios against the two types of deposits. Demand deposits expand until the initial increase of reserves provides 25 percent backing for new demand deposits—thus an increase by a factor of 4. Time deposits expand until the initial increase in reserves provides 10 percent backing for new time deposits—thus an increase by a factor of 10.

Clearly, in the real world, the result is mixed between demand and time deposits. Further, some currency begins to circulate instead of becoming bank reserves and some new currency may flow into the international economy. The real world results derived from practice are that demand deposits alone expand by a factor of 2.5, while combined demand and time deposits expand by a factor of 5. These are the expansion factors for the M_1 and M_2 definitions of money, respectively.

The Contraction Process

Bank money is contracted by exactly the inverse of the process by which it is expanded. As such, the discussion of the contraction process can be much more abbreviated than the discussion of the

Table 6-2

Money Expansion Process
(with Time Deposits)

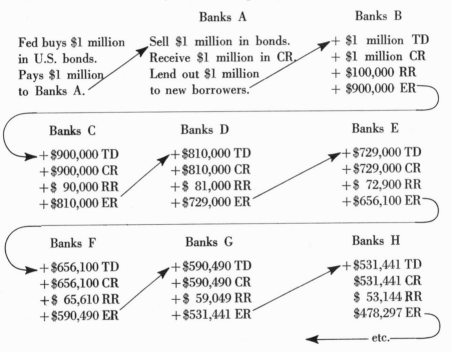

	Banks A	Banks B
Fed buys $1 million	Sell $1 million in bonds.	+ $1 million TD
in U.S. bonds.	Receive $1 million in CR.	+ $1 million CR
Pays $1 million	Lend out $1 million	+ $100,000 RR
to Banks A.	to new borrowers.	+ $900,000 ER

Banks C	Banks D	Banks E
+$900,000 TD	+$810,000 TD	+$729,000 TD
+$900,000 CR	+$810,000 CR	+$729,000 CR
+$ 90,000 RR	+$ 81,000 RR	+$ 72,900 RR
+$810,000 ER	+$729,000 ER	+$656,100 ER

Banks F	Banks G	Banks H
+$656,100 TD	+$590,490 TD	+$531,441 TD
+$656,100 CR	+$590,490 CR	$531,441 CR
+$ 65,610 RR	+$ 59,049 RR	$ 53,144 RR
+$590,490 ER	+$531,441 ER	$478,297 ER

etc.

TD = Time Deposits
CR = Cash Reserves (or equivalent Fed deposits)
RR = Dollar amount of required reserves
ER = Dollar amount of excess reserves

expansion process. To understand the contraction process, however, one must first fully understand the process of loan regeneration by banks.

At all times, some personal notes are being paid off and others issued to new borrowers. Even with a constant base of reserves this tends to happen. When banks have a reserve base of, say, $5 million, they can maintain a certain stock of outstanding demand deposits. As loans are paid off, the money paid back can be used to regenerate new loans. Frequently, loans are made on a six-month "call" basis, meaning that loans are automatically regenerated unless the bank informs the borrower that it is "calling" his loan at the end of a given six-month period.

Banks, however, do not *have* to regenerate loans. If offered a more attractive avenue for commercial activity, banks can accumulate money to purchase other kinds of assets by "calling" notes or simply by not making new loans as fast as old loans are being paid off. If, as will now be assumed, the Fed wishes to contract the money supply, it can prevent loans from being regenerated by offering an avenue for bank investments attractive enough to replace loans. This could most easily be done by offering to *sell* U. S. Government bonds through open market operations. Because the Fed is not in business to make a profit, it can offer to sell its bond holdings at however low a price it must accept in order to make the bond sale attractive.

Such a bond sale is the reverse form of open market operation necessary to expand the supply of money. As in the case of the expansion process, the discussion here will be verbal through several stages and then summarized in Table 6-3 for several additional banks, with an initial assumption that all reductions occur in the form of reduced demand deposits. Afterwards, in even more abbreviated form, a time deposit contraction process will be outlined in Table 6-4.

In order to have made a bonds purchase from the Fed, Banks A must have acquired excess reserves by the nonissuance of new loans or calling old notes. For parallel exposition, it will be assumed that the amount of the sale is $1 million, so that the Fed has given up

$1 million in U. S. Government bonds and has acquired $1 million in currency. To get that currency, Banks A must have not issued or called $1 million in loans.

As fewer loans are issued or old loans are called, demand deposits in Banks B will be reduced. In order to make payments to pay off retiring loans or called loans, individuals must draw down money holdings, here assumed to be in the form of demand deposits. Thus, Banks B will find their stable demand deposits and cash reserves falling by $1 million. At this point, their reserve ratios will drop below desired 25 percent levels. Because demand deposits have fallen by $1 million, they can afford a reduction in cash reserves of $250,000. But actual reserves have fallen by $750,000 more than this.

Banks B therefore reduce the new loans they are willing to issue and call old notes in order to acquire the $750,000 reserves they desire to replace. This implies that individuals reduce their demand deposits in Banks C in order to make payment. Banks C, in turn, find their demand deposits and cash reserves both reduced by $750,000. Of the loss of reserves, $187,500 is justified by the loss of $750,000 in demand deposits, but the remaining $562,500 is a reduction below the 25 percent level of desired reserves.

Banks C therefore begin to issue fewer new loans and call old ones in the amount of $562,500. Again, the level of demand deposits and cash reserves of Banks D must fall in consequence. Banks D find both demand deposits and cash reserves reduced by $562,500. Of the loss of cash reserves, $140,625 is justified by the loss of demand deposits and $421,875 must be gotten by the nonissuance or calling of loans. The process, as before, continues until the amounts become vanishingly small. Its continuation through Banks H is shown in Table 6-3.

At the end of the process of money contraction with assumed demand deposits reductions at each stage, the amount of reduced demand deposits will be $4 million. This is four times the initial reduction in reserves caused by the Fed's open market sale of U. S. Government bonds to the banking system. This is, of course, only a theoretical factor. In reality, the reduction factor, like the

109

Table 6-3

Money Contraction Process
(with Demand Deposits)

	Banks A	Banks B
Fed Sells $1 million in U.S. bonds. Receives $1 million from Banks A.	Buy $1 million in bonds. Give up $1 million in CR. Reduce or call loans of $1 million.	− $1 million DD − $1 million CR − $250,000 RR − $750,000 NR

Banks C	Banks D	Banks E
−$750,000 DD	−$562,500 DD	−$421,875 DD
−$750,000 CR	−$562,500 CR	−$421,875 CR
−$187,500 RR	−$140,625 RR	−$105,469 RR
−$562,500 NR	−$421,875 NR	−$316,406 NR

Banks F	Banks G	Banks H
−$316,406 DD	−$237,305 DD	−$177,979 DD
−$316,406 CR	−$237,305 CR	−$177,979 CR
−$ 79,101 RR	−$ 59,326 RR	−$ 44,495 RR
−$237,305 NR	−$177,979 NR	−$133,484 NR

——————— etc.———

DD = Demand Deposits
CR = Cash Reserves (or equivalent Fed deposits)
RR = Dollar amount of required reserves
NR = Dollar amount of needed reserves

expansion factor, would be in the neighborhood of 2.5. This is because some of the reductions would come from time deposits, some from circulating currency and some through international channels.

Contraction Through Time Deposits

If it has been assumed that reductions at each stage were financed by reducing time deposits, the reduction factor would have been 10, again paralleling the expansion process. A pure time deposit reduction assumption would mean that each time a person paid off a loan, he did so by withdrawing money from his time deposit holdings. Thus, a person who was forced to make payment on a six-month note would do so by taking money from his savings account, perhaps temporarily putting the money in his checking account, and turning the money over to the bank calling his loan.

In this case, when Banks A called loans to pay $1 million for bonds sold by the Fed, Banks B would find both cash reserves and time deposits reduced by $1 million. Of the loss of cash reserves, only 10 percent, or $100,000 would be justified because of the reduction in time deposits. Banks B would be forced to replenish $900,000 in reserves by nonissuance of new loans, or the calling of old loans.

These loans would be paid off by individuals who reduce time deposits in Banks C. As a result, Banks C have both time deposits and reserves reduced by $900,000. Of the reduction in reserves $90,000 is justified by the reduction in time deposits. Banks C must then replenish cash reserves by $810,000 in order to restore the desired 10 percent level of reserves against time deposits. This forces a calling and nonissuance of loans that reduces time deposits and cash reserves in Banks D by $810,000. The process continues until time deposits are reduced by $10 million, assuming the perfect reduction factor. This is shown for banks A to H in Table 6-4.

Reality, however, again includes a mix of demand and time

deposit reductions, some currency being removed from circulation and effects through international channels. The reduction factors for the American economy are the same as the expansion factors: 2.5 for the M_1 definition of currency in circulation plus demand deposits and 5 for the M_2 definition of currency in circulation plus demand *and* time deposits.

Powers of the Fed

The above discussion of expanding and contracting the money supply incidentally covered the workings of the most useful monetary policy tool in the arsenal of the Fed—open market operations. It also implicitly covered the workings of another extremely powerful Fed tool—the power to change reserve requirements. There are also three other important ways that the Fed can exert monetary policy on the banking system. All five will be considered in turn.

1. Open market operations. This is the purchase or sale of U. S. Government bonds and other high grade commercial paper to and from commercial banks. As has been seen above, open market sales lead to a reduction of reserves in the banking system and a corresponding reduction in the money supply. Conversely, open market purchases lead to an increase of reserves in the system and a corresponding increase in the money supply. In practice, this tool is the most useful—although not the most powerful—in the Fed's arsenal. It is so useful because it can be used to reach limited target policy objectives without drastically upsetting the system.

2. Control of reserve requirements. The Fed has the power to change reserve requirement ratios for both demand and time deposits. Since bank safety margins are based on these legal reserve requirements, a reduction in reserve requirements would lead to a reduction in bank desired reserve ratios. And, if banks reduce desired reserve ratios, reserves already in the banking system can support greater amounts of deposits. The money supply

Table 6-4

Money Contraction Process
(with Time Deposits)

	Banks A	Banks B
Fed sells $1 million in U.S. bonds. Receives $1 million from Banks A.	Buy $1 million in bonds. Give up $1 million in CR. Reduce or add loans of $1 million.	− $1 million TD − $1 million CR − $100,000 RR − $900,000 NR

Banks C	Banks D	Banks E
− $900,000 TD − $900,000 CR − $ 90,000 RR − $810,000 NR	− $810,000 TD − $810,000 CR − $ 81,000 RR − $729,000 NR	− $729,000 TD − $729,000 CR − $ 72,900 RR − $656,100 NR

Banks F	Banks G	Banks H
− $656,100 TD − $656,100 CR − $ 65,610 RR − $590,490 NR	− $590,490 TD − $590,490 CR − $ 59,049 RR − $431,441 NR	− $531,441 TD − $531,441 CR − $ 53,144 RR − $478,297 NR

——————— etc. ———————

TD = Time Deposits
CR = Cash Reserves (or equivalent Fed deposits)
RR = Dollar amount of required reserves
NR = Dollar amount of needed reserves

113

will increase. Likewise, if the Fed raises reserve requirements, bank desired reserve ratios will rise and the money supply will decline.

In its pure form, the power to change reserve requirements have seldom been used for demand deposits. The reason is that small changes in reserve requirements can have very drastic effects on the banking system. The tool is regarded as too potent for everyday use. The time deposit reserve ratio has been changed more frequently, although within limited ranges.

A special use of the power to set reserve requirements for demand deposits has been used several times in recent years. This special use depends on the existence of slightly different demand deposit reserve requirements for so called "country banks" and "city banks." It had long been felt that country banks could survive with lower demand deposit reserve requirements than could city banks. Hence, there was a difference of several percentage points in the rates the two types of banks were required to maintain. However, the definition of a "country" bank was somewhat arbitrary. Occasionally, the Fed redefined previously classified city banks as "country banks." This entitled the banks involved to lower reserve requirements and led to an expansion of the total money supply. Country banks were also occasionally reclassified as city banks in order to contract the money supply. Some medium-sized banks in medium sized cities were reclassified as both country and city banks a number of times. With the new, more complex formula for reserve requirement determination, similar policies may be followed.

3. *Setting the rediscount rate.* Another power of the Fed is the power to set the rate at which banks can borrow from the Fed. The Fed is first and foremost a banker's bank. In times of crisis, the Fed was designed to extend credit to commercial banks. But it was never expected that this credit be extended free of charge. The rate that commercial banks pay for Fed extensions of credit is called the rediscount rate. Its size is, of course, determined by the Fed on the basis of policy objectives.

Technically, the effect of lowering the rediscount rate is to make it less expensive for commercial banks to borrow from the Fed. Fed credit can be used as reserves against deposits for legal purposes and hence bank borrowing from the Fed increases the reserve base against which deposits can expand. Thus, to the degree that a lower rediscount rate provides a greater incentive for banks to borrow from the Fed, it leads to a larger money supply. Likewise, raising the rediscount makes it more expensive for commercial banks to borrow from the Fed. To the degree that this reduces bank borrowing from the Fed, reserves will decline and the money supply will contract.

In this technical economic sense, the rediscount rate is not a powerful tool. The Fed tends to regard bank borrowing from the Fed itself as evidence of the bank's weakened financial position. This, in turn, leads to a number of minor, but important, disadvantages for the bank involved. If the Fed feels that a bank is on shaky ground, it will not authorize new branches, new programs, and so forth. As such, banks tend to avoid borrowing from the Fed except when absolutely necessary. In this context, it must be realized that, under normal conditions, banks can borrow from each other. Only when they cannot do they turn to the Fed and, under such circumstances, the size of the rediscount rate is only a secondary consideration. This, of course, means that changes in the rediscount rate have only a weak effect on the size of the money supply.

There is another basically political sense in which the rediscount rate is a useful tool. In practice, the Fed is more part of the banking community than part of the government. Yet it is both. Its role is, in that sense, ambivalent. At times, the Fed acts as the representative of the banking community in government and, at other times, as the representative of government in the banking community. In this respect, changes in the rediscount rate act as political signals to the banking community.

For example, in early 1967 President Johnson had made very clear his desire for lower interest rates. In this, he had support from congressional banking committee members, notably Wright Patman. Commercial banks, however, were under considerable economic pressure to raise interest rates and Vietnam War borrowing was no small part of this. The banks were understandably cautious in going ahead with interest rate hikes that they felt were necessary. In this case, the Fed took the brunt of reaction to interest rate hikes onto itself by raising its rediscount rate. The next day, large commercial banks all over the country raised their prime interest rates. The rediscount rate change implied the Fed's blessing and the banks felt safe in going against Johnson and the Congress. On other occasions, a lowering of the rediscount rate has put pressure on the banks to do likewise with interest rates.

The rediscount rate is a potent psychological tool of the Fed.

4. Establishing selective credit controls. The Fed is empowered to establish credit limits and conditions for loans of various types by commercial banks. These take various forms and can best be explained by using several examples.

The most important example is margin requirements for stock purchase loans. Margin requirements are currently 65 percent although for a long time they were much higher than this. A margin requirement of 65 percent means that a borrower who is borrowing in order to purchase stocks as an investment must put up 65 percent of the amounts used for the stock purchase from sources other than bank loans. Only 35 percent of a stock purchase can be made through bank sources.

The reasons for margin requirements relate to the Great Depression. Prior to the Depression, individuals engaged in the practice of building financial empires by borrowing large amounts of money and investing them in the stock market. For individuals who had proven track records on this type of transaction, such loans were easily acquired prior to 1929. Some individuals had net worths of less than 10 percent of their total asset holdings.

As long as the stock market was rising rapidly, as it was in the late 1920s, individuals were able to get rich on the margins between their stock returns and the interest rates they were paying on stock acquisition loans. However, in 1929, when the stock market began dropping precipitously, the picture changed. An individual who had stock holdings of $1 million and a net worth of $100,000, coupled with loan debts of $900,000, was highly vulnerable to a downturn in the stock market. A 20 percent drop reduced the value of his stock holdings to $800,000. Since the $900,000 in debts remained, the individual's net worth became a negative $100,000. The individual was bankrupted and jumped out of a window or whatever. His bank was stuck for a loss of at least $100,000.

The bank, of course, wanted out of stocks and attempted to sell off the stocks, further depressing the stock market. This, in turn wiped out individuals whose financial positions were more secure. Again, the cycle repeated itself and the bank itself got deeper into trouble. Eventually, rumors spread and bank runs began. Many banks were ruined, as were their depositors. Here, the Fed failed to perform its function of extending credit and the banking system virtually collapsed. Between 1929 and 1933, the money supply contracted by one third. This converted what would have been a severe recession in 1929 into the most severe depression in history.

One consequence was a decision by the Congress to give power to the Fed in 1934 to set stock margin requirements—a power the Fed has had ever since.

A second example of Fed usage of selective credit controls relates to the coin shortage of 1963-65. The coin shortage itself was caused by three unrelated factors: (1) the closing of the San Francisco mint in the early 1950s; (2) the rising world price of silver that created expectations that silver content dimes, quarters and half dollars would soon be worth more as metal than as money; and (3) the rise of the vending machine, which created a much larger and previously unexpected social need for coins. The remaining mints could not run fast enough to keep up with the increasing demand. Coins were in drastic short supply, beginning in 1963, and the problem was compounded by coin hoarding.

Among other forms of coin hoarding, some individuals borrowed money from banks to invest in hoarded coins. It was a perfectly safe transaction for a bank because the coins themselves were used as collateral, locked in a safety deposit box in the bank's own vault. The Fed, however, perceived that these loan transactions were aggravating the problem of the coin shortage. A directive was therefore handed down that only 60 percent of the face value of coins could be used as loan collateral. This was designed to limit this type of coin hoarding.

So much for selective credit controls. Obviously, they limit the loan expansion process and hence hold back the expansion of the money supply.

5. The use of moral suasion. This is a polite way of saying that the Fed is powerful enough to compel "voluntary cooperation" of the banks with various unofficial policy objectives. The Fed is empowered to authorize enough different bank programs— such as setting up new branches—to give banks an incentive to cooperate with Fed policy in order to maintain good relations with the Fed. This power can be used in both an expansionary or contractionary fashion with respect to the size of the money supply.

The Effects of Debt-Created Money

In Chapters 4 and 5, the discussion of the effects of expanding and contracting the money supply was premised on the assumption that the money involved was not created by debt. Here, all of the tools of the Fed involve mechanisms of money creation that also involve debt creation. In this sense, any dollar created through the banking system is matched by the creation of a dollar in debts somewhere in the system. This is true whether the change comes about because of open-market operations, changes in reserve requirements or in other Fed policies. Since, in fact, most money created in the American economy is created in this way, it is important to consider the differences debt creation or reduction makes in the impact of monetary changes.

For a book of this sort, the slightly different effects of creating money through changing reserve requirements as compared to creating money through open market operations are not crucial. For simplicity, they will be ignored. But one conclusion about debt creation of money must not be ignored. If each dollar created is matched by a dollar of debt, the earlier conclusions about the interest rate in the adjustment process must be modified.

In an economic sense, the personal notes issued as money expands or not issued as money contracts are forms of bonds. Clearly, their existence or nonexistence affects the interest rate prevailing in the economy. When money expands, the supply of bonds (including notes) rises by more than if the money were created without debt creation. The initial fall in interest rates will be steeper and while the rate will tend to rise in the later stages of the adjustment process, it will not return to its initial level. It will remain permanently lower. And, because the rate of return on real assets must equal the interest rate in the long run, that rate will also remain permanently lower.

Conversely, when money contracts in a way that reduces debt, the supply of bonds falls by more than if the money were eliminated without debt reduction. The initial rise in interest rates will be steeper and while the rate will tend to fall back in the later stages of the adjustment process, it will not return to its initial level. It will remain permanently higher. And, again, because the rate of return on real assets must equal the interest rate in the long run, that rate will also remain permanently lower.

With this qualification, the discussion now moves to how this information can be utilized for investment purposes.

Chapter Seven

Monetarism and Investment

There is no way that monetarism can be translated into a simple formula for investment success. It cannot act as a theory for selecting individual stocks, bonds, land or other asset holdings. That is not what will be attempted here. What monetarism can do for the investor is to give him a better basis for expecting future changes in the economy. It can also provide a basis for choosing between stocks in general and bonds in general under certain types of circumstances. It is the purpose of this chapter to concentrate on those aspects of the investment process.

It will not do so by an in depth discussion of forecasting techniques a monetarist might use. That has been done elsewhere by professional forecasters and economists with more experience in forecasting than this author.* Instead, the purpose here is to

---

* See Beryl Sprinkel, *Money and Markets: A Monetarist View* (Homewood, Ill.: Richard D. Irwin, 1971); and A. James Meigs, *Money Matters: Economics, Markets, Politics* (New York: Harper and Row, 1972).

give the reader a basis for making intuitive judgments of the future by using readily available information. The assumption here is that the reader is willing to keep abreast of certain types of financial information, but that he does not intend to sit down and work out involved analytic forecasts. What is really involved in this chapter, then, is a discussion of how to get and use monetary information for investing.

Sources of Monetary Information

The primary sources of information about monetary data are in the Federal Reserve System. This is important for the investor to realize because the normal news media does not understand the importance of monetary information and does not report this information on a normal basis. *Barron's, The Wall Street Journal* and other special financial media are somewhat better in this respect, but are still somewhat inadequate in monetary reporting. Fortunately, information from the Federal Reserve System is free of charge upon request. One need only to write to the Federal Reserve Board in Washington or to the appropriate individual federal reserve bank and request the publication in question. One does *not* have to live within a given Federal Reserve District to receive information from a federal reserve bank.

Each individual federal reserve bank has its own publications and its own philosophy. There are twelve such banks, located in Boston, Chicago, Cleveland, Minneapolis, Kansas City, San Francisco, New York, Dallas, Atlanta, Philadelphia, Richmond and St. Louis. Of these, only the St. Louis Federal Reserve Bank has a basically monetarist outlook.* The publications of the St. Louis Fed are thus most useful to the individual investor. The one other important Fed source of information is the *Federal Reserve Bulletin,* a monthly publication of the Federal Reserve Board in Washington. The Appendix provides an excellent discussion by Homer

---

* A very recent development may change this. Michael Keran, the new research director of the San Francisco Fed, has distinct monetarist leanings and learned his trade at the St. Louis Fed.

Jones on how to use these information sources. Homer Jones is a former vice president of the St. Louis Fed and was instrumental in developing the data reporting system now in use.

With these sources and Jones's remarks, any investor can become a reasonably sophisticated observer of monetary changes.

The greatest problem in using monetary data for investment purposes is the variety of patterns that are found in practice. The Fed has traditionally followed a variety of policies and these sometimes have changed suddenly from month to month. The effects of these changes have, of course, depended on their nature and strength. The possibilities are endless. Yet certain types of patterns can be discussed and their effects considered for general characteristics. Each possibility has been, in effect, already considered in either Chapter 4 or Chapter 5, but not with a focus on specific developments at specific points in time. Here, the objective is to establish categories of patterns, to indicate the types and timing of effects and to note possible investment objectives in each situation. Deflationary patterns will be ignored for lack of relevance. The patterns to be considered in turn will be:

1. Stable Noninflationary Monetary Growth. This would be a situation in which two conditions are met. The rate of increase in the money supply is relatively constant from month to month. It is also a rate that is equal to or slightly greater than the rate of real economic growth.

2. Unstable Noninflationary Monetary Growth. In this situation, the long run rate of increase in the money supply is approximately equal to the rate of real economic growth. But on a month-to-month basis, the rate of change varies considerably.

3. Stable Inflationary Monetary Growth. Here, the rate of increase in the money supply is relatively constant from month to month. It is, however, a rate that is enough larger than the rate of real economic growth to produce a rate of inflation.

4. Unstable Inflationary Monetary Growth. The rate of increase in the money supply varies widely from month to month, but the long run rate of increase is large enough to produce inflation.

After dealing with each of these patterns, the effects of shifting from one pattern to another will be considered.

Stable Noninflationary Monetary Growth

When the money supply is being increased at a relatively constant rate that approximates the rate of real economic growth, the price level will remain relatively constant. Expectations of changes in the price level will be absent and economic planning by individuals and firms will not be disrupted by an inability to complete plans at expected costs. Such slight inflations and recessions as might occur would be caused by nonmonetary factors. And, according to monetarist theory, these economic problems would be minor in impact. The economy as a whole would stay near a state of full economic adjustment with rates of increase in both demand and supply approximately similar in all markets. In short, the economy would remain in a basically sound condition.

In such a situation, investment decisions should be made purely on the basis of other than monetary factors. High grade bonds would be almost perfectly secure investments while stock equities and land would be more risky because of less certain future performances. Their rates will reflect this risk in higher expected rates of return and investors can choose the degree of risk they are willing to bear in a fairly straightforward fashion. If this situation were in evidence in the real world, this book would not have been written.

Unstable Noninflationary Monetary Growth

From 1950 to 1964, the price level increased at an annual rate of approximately 1 percent per year. This, however, was the *measured* rate of inflation and many economists believe that a 1 percent rate of inflation is equivalent to a truly constant price level. Inflation, in any case, was not a serious problem during this period. Yet, it was hardly a period of perfect monetary stability. There

124

were two recessions (1954 and 1959) and several periods during which inflation at least loomed as a threat. Such a period can be characterized as the consequences of "unstable noninflationary monetary growth." Over the long term, the rate of increase in the money supply was slightly faster than the rate of real economic growth, but on a month to month basis, it varied significantly.

In such a situation, all economic calculations become less certain than in the stable monetary growth situation. This, of course, complicates the investor's problems if he prefers to minimize risk. Fluctuations in bond prices become more significant. Only by holding bonds to maturity can the investor be as safe in bonds as in the previous case. But at the same time, the opportunities for the investor who can reasonably interpret monetary changes may be increased.

The long run effect of unstable noninflationary monetary growth is similar to that of stable noninflationary monetary growth in terms of expectations of price level changes. The primary difference between stable and unstable noninflationary monetary growth is that monetary instability, by disrupting economic plans of both firms and individuals, leads to a greater wastage of resources. This, in turn, leads to a somewhat smaller real output of goods and services.

In the long run, rates of return on stocks and bonds and other assets will tend to remain constant, given noninflationary monetary growth. But instability may cause these rates to vary significantly in the short run. And corresponding to rate fluctuations will be fluctuations in asset prices. The wise investor can use his knowledge of monetary changes to judge the timing of his purchases in such a way as to minimize purchase prices and maximize selling prices—at least in a general way. Buying stocks and bonds shortly after a monetary decline, for example, is wise. So is selling shortly after a monetary increase in this situation.

It is important to take this kind of suggestion in the proper light. There is no way that rapid buying and selling of stocks on the basis of short-term monetary changes can be called sound investing—any more than any other kind of short term buying and selling. That is not suggested here. What is suggested is that the timing of purchases and sales decided upon by other factors be considered in light of monetary changes. When an investor has decided to buy a given stock on the basis of a thorough consideration of the company, he must then choose *when* to buy. Any natural cycles in the stock's price should be considered, but so should prior monetary changes.

In this, again, the investor must be careful. The timing of any one month's effects is not perfectly predictable. Further, the effect of one month's changes may be cancelled out by changes in the next month. Only when changes in any one direction have continued for several months can reasonable use be made of this type of calculation. And, secondly, for this type of calculation to be accurate, the trend must reverse itself within less than a year. If it does not, the economy will shift patterns away from unstable noninflationary nonmonetary growth into either deflationary or inflationary conditions, depending on the direction—up or down—in the rate of change in the money supply.

But if these conditions are met, several months after a *relative* decline in monetary growth begins, individuals will find themselves holding less cash balances than they desire. This will cause them to seek to replenish cash holdings initially by selling or not buying assets. At this point asset prices will fall, but the fall will be temporary and will eventually disappear as effects occur in other parts of the economy. As discussed in Chapter 5, this effect will occur first in bond prices and shortly thereafter in stock prices. Land prices will also tend to fall, but are less responsive to this type of change.

The specific timing will depend on the strength and consistency of the monetary decline, as will other nonmonetary factors. This the investor must judge for himself, but some general guidelines are possible. These are:

1. Unless the monetary decline continues for several months, it will be difficult to detect any noticeable effect on asset prices.

2. If there is good reason to expect that the declines will continue, the effects described here should be considered in light of other effects to be described later in the chapter.

3. The steeper the relative monetary declines, the stronger the price effects are likely to be.

4. Price declines are likely to continue for several months after they begin. The investor should not be anxious to become involved as soon as effects begin to appear.

5. In stock prices, where price increases are part of the return to investors, the effects will not necessarily be price declines, but may be more slowly rising prices.

6. In general, the best time to buy may range from several months to a year after a noticeable monetary growth decline can be observed.

7. There is no substitute for good judgment of a company in buying either stocks or bonds.

Likewise, within the conditions of this discussion, a relative increase in monetary growth will cause individuals to find themselves holding excess cash balances. They will seek to dispose of these balances by buying other assets, thus bidding up asset prices. This price rise will be temporary and will afford an investor the chance to sell assets he had previously decided to sell at higher than normal prices. As covered in Chapter 4, these price rises will eventually disappear as other effects in other parts of the economy cause reverse pressure in asset prices.

The guidelines for selling to take advantage of these changes are essentially similar to those for buying after a monetary decline except that changes appear likely to occur more quickly after a monetary increase than after a decline. They are:

1. Unless the monetary expansion continues for several months, it will be difficult to detect any noticeable effect on asset prices.

2. If there is good reason to expect that the expansion will continue, the effects described here should be considered in light of other effects to be described later in the chapter.

3. The steeper the relative monetary increases, the stronger the price effects are likely to be.

4. Price increases are likely to go on for several months after they begin.

5. In general, the best time to sell may range from several months to a year after a noticeable monetary growth increase can be observed.

6. Again, there is no substitute for good business judgment in either buying or selling.

Stable Inflationary Monetary Growth

Like stable *non*inflationary growth, stable inflationary monetary growth is seldom (if ever) found in the real world. It would occur only if the growth rate in the supply of money were stable on a month-to-month basis, but at a rate at least 1 percent greater than the rate of real economic growth. In this circumstance, the price level would be rising by slightly less than the difference between the rate of monetary increase and the rate of real economic growth. But it would be rising at a constant rate that would be predicted by all parties to economic transactions. As such, the economy would maintain itself in what would be regarded as sound condition except for the inflation itself.

In this situation, inflation would present no special problem for investor planning. Bond prices would be stable, but with market interest rates that included both real interest and an inflationary premium equal to the expected (and actual) rate of inflation. Real asset prices would be rising at a rate that fully compensated for the rate of inflation as well as productivity increases. Contracts in other markets of the economy would be made with the rate of inflation fully accounted for. Once the economy became fully geared to the existing rate of inflation, that rate of inflation would do very little damage to the economy. As with stable noninflationary monetary growth, monetary factors could essentially be ignored for investment purposes.

Unstable Inflationary Monetary Growth

With unstable inflationary monetary growth, real world applications are easy to find—the present being a prime example. In this situation, some amount of inflation is expected, but the rate itself is uncertain within a certain range. Relative increases and decreases in the money supply, as compared to the general trend, will exert influences on the economy that closely parallel the effects in monetary changes of unstable noninflationary growth. But they also have other effects on the relative attractiveness of stocks and bonds that could be considered.

Since 1965, the United States has been subject to inflation that has ranged between 3 and 6 percent annually. Periodically, during this time, new initiatives to halt inflation have been undertaken and those attempts that involved monetary control have had an impact on the economy. Yet, before any policy that would have worked has had time to take affect, it has been reversed and the inflationary path has been restored. The pattern is unmistakable and it is likely to continue for at least the next several years— mostly because of a misunderstanding of monetary effects. No monetary problem can be cleared up in a few months and policies that are right in emphasis are frequently so strong in character that they cause the twin problem of recession. In the next chapter, programs for correcting the present impasse will be discussed. In this one, the emphasis is on how the investor can cope with such a situation.

The first effect to be considered is the increased riskiness of bonds relative to real assets. Bond interest rates, as was discussed in Chapter 2, tend to reflect the rate of expected inflation. When that rate is relatively certain, as it is with a stable but inflationary rate of monetary growth, bonds are as inflation "proof" as real assets. It is only when inflation is unexpected or the amount of it is uncertain that bonds become prone to lose value during inflations. This is because bonds are, in one way or another, fixed in money terms and these fixed money terms cannot respond to unexpected inflationary changes. Bonds gain value when inflation is unexpectedly small and lose value when it is unexpectedly large. This is the risk factor that develops in bonds with unstable inflationary monetary growth.

Equities are always risky to one degree or another because their future values are not fixed in money terms. Because of this, however, their prices are free to adjust upwards during prolonged inflations, as can their dividends in the case of stock equities. The commonly held view that equities are inflation-proof is exaggerated, but it is at least true that equities *can* adjust for unexpected inflationary changes. That is not true of bonds.

The basic point here is *not* that bonds become more risky than stocks in some absolute sense. It is rather that bonds increase their degree of risk *more* than do stocks under conditions of inflationary uncertainty. As such, the security advantage of bonds declines somewhat relative to stocks, and bond prices will begin to reflect risk compensations, meaning that interest rates rise somewhat more than rates of return on equities when this condition develops. This, of course, implies that bond prices will fall. Being aware of this is the first problem of the investor in this situation.

The second set of effects to be considered are those that closely parallel under unstable noninflationary monetary growth. After relative monetary increases (monetary increases faster than the general trend), the first effects to appear will be asset price rises faster than the previous trend. If it can be expected that the deviation from trend is temporary and likely to reverse itself later, these relative asset prices rises will be temporary. If an investor is planning to sell assets, this would be a good time.

After a relative monetary decline (monetary increases slower than the general trend), the first effects to appear would be asset price declines or increases slower than the previous trend. If it can be expected that the deviation from trend is temporary and likely to reverse itself later, these relative asset price declines will be temporary. If an investor is planning to buy assets, this would be a good time.

Guidelines for both possibilities would be:

1. Unless the monetary deviation from trend continues for several months, it will be difficult to detect any noticeable effect on asset prices.

2. If there is good reason to expect that the changes will be maintained in the same direction, the effects described here should be considered in light of other effects to be described later in the chapter.

3. The stronger the shifts from trend, the stronger the price effects are likely to be.

4. Asset price effects in the appropriate direction are likely to go on for several months after they begin.

5. In equity prices, including stocks, relative declines may lead to more slowly rising asset prices after relative declines instead of absolute price reductions.

6. Bond price changes will tend to occur before equity prices.

7. Price effects following relative monetary increases will tend to occur sooner than price effects of relative monetary declines, but both types of effects will tend to begin to occur within a range of several months to a year.

The Effects of Transitional Changes

Each of the previous discussions was premised on the assumption that a given pattern of monetary changes was in evidence. All guidelines for investment activity were based on that assumption. Yet, clearly patterns do in fact change, the most recent example being a shift from a pattern of unstable noninflationary monetary growth to a pattern of unstable inflationary monetary growth in 1964-65.

Such basic changes do not occur frequently, but they occur often enough that an investor should be aware of the possibility of such shifts. It is also important to realize that the difference between a short term instability and a long term trend depends on one's definition of "long term." In the way these terms have been used here, the 1954 and 1959-60 recessions were caused by short term relative declines in monetary growth. The Johnson-Nixon Great Inflation is a long term trend that began in 1964-65. Any shift from general patterns that irons itself out in a period of two years or less and returns to the previous pattern would be called an "instability." Any shift that goes on longer than that would be called a "transition" to a new pattern.

This distinction is obviously arbitrary. The longer that a short-term shift from basic patterns continues, the more like a transition it becomes. Even so, a true transitional change has important implications for the behavior of economic variables—and of investors. In this sense, transitional periods can be classified in two groups: upward and downward adjustments in price level expectations. These will be considered in turn.

Upward Adjustments in Price Level Expectations

An upward adjustment in price level expectations can begin from a deflationary, constant or inflationary price level trend. What is required is that the price level at various points in the future be higher than it was expected to be by economic decision makers. This could be accomplished by a deflationary movement less deflationary than it was expected to be, by an inflationary movement when the price level was expected to be constant, or by an inflationary movement more inflationary than it was expected to be.

When an upward adjustment begins, the difference between expectations and actual results sets in motion the process of adjustment described in Chapter 4, with all markets ultimately being affected. This set of effects would occur following any upward deviation from a prevailing monetary trend and if counteracted later becomes nothing more than an instability, with the affects and investment advice discussed earlier. But if it continues long enough, expectations themselves begin to change and a secondary set of effects will occur. The transition period itself is the period during which individual and firm expectations are catching up with actual price level results. Once they have, a new pattern has set in, with the effects described earlier in this chapter for that pattern. In terms of the Johnson-Nixon Great Inflation, this transition period lasted from 1965 to 1967.

The transition period is thus a period which begins with changes that are regarded as instabilities and ends with the same kind of changes being regarded as normal and typical. In the process, the initial effects that are observed reverse themselves into almost precisely the opposite effects. It will be useful to follow these steps carefully. In doing so, the earlier distinction between stable and unstable trends can largely be ignored because the transition period itself is inherently unstable.

In the first stage, the money supply begins to increase faster than expectations would warrant. Individuals and firms find themselves holding larger than desired cash balances. They try to use these excess cash balances to purchase assets, which temporarily drives up asset prices and drives down rates of return, including the interest rate. This spreads the force of excess money to the goods market where prices relatively and output absolutely begin to rise. The falling interest rate and other rates of returns, coupled with a more rapidly rising price level, would now tend to restore full adjustment in the money market in the manner seen earlier— except for one thing. Excess money continues to flow into the money market on the supply side.

This continued creation of money in excess of amounts warranted by expectations and hence plans of individuals and firms leads to a continuation of effects. For a time, therefore, the interest rate and other rates of return will continue to fall and the price level continues to rise at an accelerated rate. During *this* period, real assets and especially stock equities have a significant advantage over bonds to the investor. This is because returns in stocks will be rising along with asset prices, while the absolute amount of interest on bonds to original purchasers remains fixed. Those holding bonds are losing value to inflation, while those holding stock equities *may* not be doing so, depending on the degree of confidence in the economy—to be sure, a nonmonetary variable.

This period of continuing declines in the interest rate and other rates of return, however, can only last as long as the long term trend is not realized by a majority of investors. It will happen as long as investors and borrowers continue to expect that the economy will return to its previous trend. Once it becomes obvious that this is not the case and that the more rapid rate of inflation (or less rapid deflation in that unworldly possibility) has become the normal trend, things will change. Investors, now expecting the higher rate of inflation, will plan accordingly. They will demand rates of return and an interest rate that compensates them for the losses they would otherwise suffer from the more rapid inflation. At this point, the interest rate and other rates of return reverse their previous trends, eliminating previous declines and move to higher rates than before the transition began. This change from rates that were lower than before the transition began to rates that are higher can be quite dramatic, as it was in 1967. It will normally occur in the second year after a transition begins.

The earlier advice in this chapter—about selling several months after an unstable increase in the money supply occurs— must be modified in light of this. Though the value of assets may be higher for a year and a half after an inflationary transition begins, bond values will eventually fall significantly as interest rates rise. Stock values, however, are largely exempt from this effect because returns on stocks will also be rising, so that the now higher rate of return on stocks (including appreciation) is not achieved by falling asset prices, but by rising returns. Stock equities are much safer than bonds during such a period.

Once expectations have caught up with actual rates of change in the price level, the economy will have restored itself to a new pattern and the previous advice begins to hold again. The economy is back in either a stable or unstable inflationary monetary growth pattern.

Downward Adjustment in Price Level Expectations

A downward adjustment in price level expectations can, like an upward adjustment, begin from a deflationary, constant or inflationary price level trend. What is required is that the price level at various points in the future be lower than it was expected to be by economic decision makers. This could be accomplished by a deflationary movement more deflationary than it was expected to be, by a deflationary movement when the price level was expected to be constant, or by an inflationary movement less inflationary than it was expected to be.

When a downward adjustment begins the difference between expectations and actual results sets in motion the process of adjustment described in Chapter 5, with all markets being affected as the process proceeds. This process is, at the outset, similar to the set of events that would occur following any downward deviation from a prevailing monetary trend and if counteracted later becomes nothing more than an instability, with the effects and investment advice discussed earlier. But if the effects continue long enough, expectations themselves begin to change and a secondary set of effects will occur. The transition period itself is the period during which individual and firm expectations are adjusting to actual price level results. When expectations have become consistent with events, a new pattern has set in. This new pattern will have the effects described earlier in the chapter for that pattern. Such a transition period occurred at the outset of the Great Depression and will be required for an end of the present inflationary trend, although hopefully with less disastrous results. How that might be accomplished will be discussed in the next chapter.

The transition period begins with changes that are regarded as instabilities and ends with the same kinds of changes being regarded as normal and typical. In the process, the initial effects that are observed reverse themselves into almost precisely the opposite effects. In going through the steps in this process, it's possible to ignore largely the earlier distinction between stable and unstable trends because the transition period itself is inherently unstable.

In the first stage, the money supply begins to increase faster than expectations would warrant. Individuals and firms find themselves holding smaller than desired cash balances. They try to restore desired cash balances by selling assets, which temporarily drives down asset prices and ups the interest rate and other rates of return. This spreads the force of monetary shortage to the goods market where prices begin to fall or rise less rapidly and output begins to fall. A recession is set in motion. The rising interest rate and other rates of return, coupled with a falling or more slowly rising price level, would now tend to restore full adjustment in the money market in the case of an instability. Here, however, the relative declines in the money supply are continuing and the money shortage is perpetuated.

This continued monetary shortage continues to disrupt individual and firm planning and leads to a continuation of effects. For a time, therefore, the interest rate and other rates of return will continue to rise and prices continue to fall or rise less rapidly. During this stage, bonds have a significant advantage over real assets to the investor. This is because returns on stocks will be falling along with asset prices, while the absolute amount of interest on bonds to original purchasers remains fixed. Those holding bonds are gaining value through *relative* deflation, which is probably not true of those holding stock equities, depending on the degree of confidence in the economy.

This period of continuing rises in the interest rate and other rates of return, however, can only last as long as investors and borrowers continue to expect that the economy will return to its previous trend. Once it becomes obvious that this is not the case and that the deflation or less rapid inflation has become the normal trend, some effects will reverse themselves. Investors, now expecting a lower rate of inflation, will plan accordingly. They will accept a lower interest and lower rates of return because the real value of any given return is now higher. At this point, the interest rate and other rates of return reverse their previous rises and begin to fall to levels lower than before the transition began. This change from rates that were higher than before the transition began to rates that are lower can be quite dramatic, as it was in 1930. It will normally occur in the second year after a transition begins.

The earlier advice in this chapter—about selling several months after an unstable relative decline in the money supply

136

occurs—must be modified in this situation. The value of assets may be lower for a year and a half after an inflationary transition begins, but bond values will eventually rise as interest rates finally fall. Stock values, on the other hand, will not have this advantage because returns on stocks will also be falling. This means that the eventually lower rate of return on stocks (including depreciation, if any) is not achieved by rising asset prices, buy by falling returns. Bonds have a true advantage in this situation.

Again, once expectations have caught up with actual rates of change in the price level, the economy will have restored itself to a new pattern. The previous advice begins to hold again because the economy has returned to one of the patterns discussed earlier in the chapter.

Chapter Eight

A Program for Reform

This has not been a book that is favorable to the past policies of the Federal Reserve System. In practice, the Fed has been and is a source of unnecessary instability in the economy. It is likely to continue having such an impact as long as it maintains its central role in the money supply process. The purpose of this chapter is to explain why Fed policy tends to be erratic even to the point of causing the Great Depression of 1929-38 and the Johnson-Nixon Great Inflation that began in 1965 and continues today. It will be suggested that even wise Fed policy would be inferior to an alternative system in which the Fed had no control over the money supply. That system will be explained and some of its hidden advantages pointed out.

The Instability of Fed Policy Making

In practice, the Fed has followed a number of different policy orientations since its inception in 1914. At times it has been somewhat monetarist in its orientation and at other times has appeared to be almost unconcerned about monetary variables altogether, concentrating instead on short-term interest rates. Board members have changed, as have their philosophies. Nothing has been consistent about Fed policy over time except its inconsistency. This has led to situations such as occurred prior to the 1970 recession where after rapidly increasing the money supply for several years, the Fed suddenly stopped all monetary growth for a period of seven months. Then, when it became obvious that the recession this caused was in the offing, the Fed immediately reverted to rapid expansion. The consequence was a recession that produced very little inflationary relief.

In other situations, the Fed has turned its attention to the interest rate structure. In the early 1960s, it followed a policy, dubbed in financial circles as "Operation Twist," in which the focus was on an attempt to produce high short term interest rates and low long-term interest rates. The philosophy behind this was that high short term rates would attract foreign money and ease balance of payments difficulties, while low long-term rates would induce more rapid capital investment. The only way this would have been accomplished would have caused a recession. Fortunately, in this case, the policy was largely ineffective in terms of its objectives. At other times the Fed has been more successful and the economy has suffered.

The "whys" are perhaps hidden in the minds of members of the Federal Reserve Board. The consequences are on the record and there is only one way to describe them—money mismanagement.

The Great Depression

The greatest of the Fed's mistakes was the Great Depression. It has caused other recessions and it has now caused significant inflations, but no single economic event has had a negative economic and psychological impact on the economy equal to that of the Depression. Only today, forty years later, are individuals recovering the self-confidence that their own economic survivals depend more on their own efforts than that of government.

The Great Depression began in 1929 as a recession of the sort the Fed has periodically caused in the course of its existence. It would have been a moderately severe recession, but certainly nothing like what actually happened if it had not been for complicating factors. After the recession was already underway, the stock market began to suffer the steepest declines in its history. The Fed's reaction to the stock market crash was to maintain a contractionary pressure on the money supply. This deepened the recession and supported continued stock market declines. By 1931, the recession had become more than a recession—a depression that matched previous depressions in American history. But it still had not taken the one step that would set it aside as the greatest economic disaster in American history.

That step involved the virtual collapse of the banking system. Since many bank loans were backed with stock collateral, the stock market declines were eating up the collateral base of banks. Borrowers who were depending on stock values to make payment on these loans were unable to do so. Banks had to foreclose the loans and sell the stocks for whatever they could get. This had two effects. First, it increased the supply of stocks on the stock market and further depressed stock prices. Second, banks themselves got further and further into financial difficulty.

Some banks were bankrupted and a bank panic began. Reserves flowed out of the banking system. At this point, the Fed confounded its earlier mistakes by refusing to extend credit to commercial banks in need of reserves. This action was contrary to one of the primary purposes of the Fed, but the Fed apparently felt that unwise bank practice in loan creation was at fault for what had happened and refused to make reserves available to the banks. With all of this going on, the money supply continued to contract. By 1933, the money supply had declined to two thirds of its 1929 pre-Depression levels.

After 1933, the money supply slowly began to increase again and the economy slowly began to recover. This recovery was seriously interrupted again in 1937 by another spate of bank failures, again caused by Fed inaction, but the severity was far less than what had happened earlier. By 1940, the Depression had ended and America began backing into World War II.

Several points are important. The Fed's responsibility was paramount. It caused the recession with monetary declines in 1929. It turned the recession into a depression with continuing monetary declines. And it made the depression the worst in America's history by its refusal to extend credit to commercial banks. The Great Depression itself was thus a consequence of a series of mistakes and not one simple wrong move. But all of the mistakes can be laid at the Fed's doorstep.

The Great Inflation

The Johnson-Nixon Great Inflation has not been of the same order of magnitude as the Great Depression, but it has been the second worst failure of the Fed. Like the Great Depression, the Great Inflation began innocuously enough. The troop buildup for the Vietnam War, which began in early 1965, was accompanied by a growing deficit in the federal budget. Probably to facilitate government borrowing, the Fed began to create money at a rate that would eventually support 5 percent inflation. The rate was about 9 percent annually. Initially, this had the desired effect of lowering the interest rates at which the government had to borrow. But, by 1967, inflationary expectations began to set in. Interest rates reversed their earlier declines and began to rise to all-time highs.

Through the latter half of 1967 and the first eleven months of 1968, the Fed continued to push monetary expansion, perhaps hoping to force interest rates back down. In December 1968, the

142

Fed embarked on a tight money policy. Whether this would have continued under the Fed chairmanship of William McChesney Martin will never be known. Shortly after President Nixon's inauguration, Martin resigned, apparently with the understanding that Arthur F. Burns would be his replacement. Nixon wanted a man who was committed to monetary restraint and Burns certainly fit that bill.

Under Burns, the monetary restraint was tightened even more and from May to December of 1969, the money supply did not increase at all. This made a recession inveitable. When it began to manifest itself in early 1970, the Fed reversed itself and began to rapidly increase the money supply, thereby regenerating inflationary fires. Since then, the Fed has been increasing the money supply rapidly enough to maintain a slowly declining rate of inflation. As of the moment that this is being written, it is again following severe restraint. Another recession looms unless this policy is reversed. On that, the future will tell.

It is, however, likely that such a severe contractionary policy would be reversed at the inception of a new recession. If so, the economy would again suffer a recession without much inflation abatement. It is to be feared that such reactions and counter-reactions will continue for some period of time into the future—until monetarism is better understood.

The Problem of Discretionary Policy

Even if the Fed had a proper policy orientation, its policy decisions would probably do more harm than good. There are inherent difficulties in monetary policy decision-making that no amount of understanding can solve. These exist because of time lags in acquiring information about the economy and in implementing monetary policy after information is obtained. If the Fed had a crystal ball, it might be able to benefit the economy by foreseeing fluctuations in output caused by nonmonetary factors and adjusting monetary policy to benefit the economy. Just what it would be appropriate to have the Fed do under such circumstances is a tricky question. But since this is academic, it need not concern us. The Fed does not have such a crystal ball and the question is irrelevant to the real world.

Since it does not, its actions must be based on guesses about the future. Data about the economy is only available on a quarterly basis to any accurate degree. And, quarterly data is available only after a lag of a month. Thus, facts about the first month of a quarter are only accurately available three months after it ends. The Fed does not know the present accurately, let alone the future. On top of this, the effect of monetary changes, as has been seen earlier, is by no means immediate. The effect of any one month's changes in the money supply only *start being noticeable* from six to nine months later and continue for some time thereafter. What frequently happens when the Fed occasionally tries to use the appropriate policy is that the policy which would have been correct for the time adopted is absolutely wrong for the time when it takes effect.

Fixed Rules in Monetary Policy

The meaning of all this is that the Fed simply cannot, even if determined to do so, follow an effective *discretionary* monetary policy. Knowing and implementing the appropriate policy at each stage of economic change is simply not possible in an uncertain world in which economic developments are the consequences of human decisions. Given this impossibility, Milton Friedman has argued for a *fixed rule* monetary policy. Such a fixed rule policy would involve increasing the money supply at a constant rate, selected for some specified long-term period.

The advantages of a fixed rule policy is that while policy would rarely be perfect, it would seldom be far from correct. The economy tends to grow at a relatively constant long-run rate. Further, most of the present short-term fluctuations in the growth rate originate in the money market from money supply disturbances. With a constant rate of increase in the money supply, this source of fluctuations would disappear and the growth rate itself would be more stable. It is, of course, true that there are other causes of economic fluctuations than monetary disturbances. These would continue even if the money supply were being increased at a constant rate, but nonmonetary disturbances have not been serious under normal circumstances. Such fluctuations as would occur with constant monetary rates of change would not produce serious economic problems. These, a monetarist would argue, can be lived with.

With a fixed rule monetary policy, the constant rate of change in the money supply would produce a relatively constant rate of change in the price level. The price level would vary slightly due to changes in nonmonetary factors, but these variations would be slight and would even out in the long run. This would cause individual expectations about future price level changes to be accurate enough not to disrupt economic plans. Investments, in general, would be safer in such a circumstance although windfall gains would be less frequent. The economy itself would seldom enter recessions and those it did enter would be minor in character.

It is important to note that *any* rate of change in the money supply, if constantly maintained, would produce this result. If the rate of monetary growth is greater than the rate of output growth at least by one percent, the price level will be rising at a constant rate equal to or slightly less than the differences. If the rate of monetary growth is smaller than the rate of output growth, the price level will be falling at a constant rate slightly greater than the difference. If the rate of monetary growth is equal to (or slightly greater than) the rate of output growth, the price level will remain approximately constant. But whether the price level is inflationary, deflationary or remaining constant, if it is doing so at a constant rate, individual and firm decisions will not be disrupted by inaccurate predictions about the future. The economy can fully adjust to any continuing price level trend.

145

Implementation of Fixed Rules

It would be possible to have the Congress instruct the Fed to increase the money supply at a constant rate. There are, however, several reasons why this would not be the most expeditious method of implementing a fixed rule monetary policy. For one thing, the money expansion process has a variable length of duration. The present expansion process depends on loan creation by commercial banks. The rate at which loans are created is not a constant, but depends on prevailing economic conditions. For this reason, it would be difficult for the Fed to prevent fluctuations in the rate of monetary growth.

Secondly, with the appropriate institutional adjustments, there is no good reason for the increases in the money stock to be accomplished through the banking system at all. And there are some important gains to be made in the fiscal process of government if appropriate institutional changes are, in fact, made—a matter of $20 billion or more. The source of this savings will be considered after discussing the proposal for 100 percent reserves for demand deposits in the banking system.

The Case for 100 Percent Reserves

In the financial system of the United States, only commercial banks are permitted to create demand deposits. This limitation has been a very significant advantage for commercial banks over other forms of financial institutions. Through being able to lend out money derived from demand deposits, banks have had a tremendous profitability advantage over their nonbank financial competitors. The proposal for 100 percent reserves begins with an argument that financial markets could be made more competitive by eliminating this advantage of commercial banks.

With 100 percent reserves, banks would have to maintain

146

reserves equal to the amount of their outstanding demand deposits. This would mean that banks would become, in essence, a warehouse for currency and could not lend out any part of amounts deposited in demand deposits. Time deposits are a different matter and *all* financial institutions would continue to be permitted to lend out a large fraction of amounts deposited on time. Time deposits and not demand deposits would be a source of handling capital for banks and other financial institutions.

Under 100 percent reserves, the money supply would be equal to the amount of currency in existence. The arguments for the M₂ definitions of money would vanish because banks would no longer have any incentive to pay interest on demand deposits. Indeed, charges for checking privileges would go up, which is one of the primary disadvantages of the system. There would thus be no confusion about deposit types and the M₁ definition could be relied upon. The M₁ definition, again, is currency in circulation plus demand deposits. Demand deposits would equal currency in reserves. The remaining currency would be in circulation. Hence the money supply would simply equal the amount of existing currency.

This would eliminate another potential source of monetary instability from the monetary system. Now, the ratio between currency in circulation to currency in reserves has a key role in determining the size of the money supply. Money taken out of circulation and put into reserves expands by a factor of 2½ by the M₁ definition under the present system. This means that individual decisions about the *form* of money holdings can have a significant impact on the *size* of the money supply. In practice, this is less important than it might seem because the ratio of currency in circulation to currency in reserves has tended to remain fairly stable. Still, whatever amount of instability it produces would be eliminated under 100 percent reserves. There would be no expansion factor as currency moved out of circulation and into reserves.

147

The Case for Fiat Currency

A second institutional shift that would be appropriate would be a basic change in the form of currency. At present, most U.S. currency is in the form of Federal Reserve Notes, which are technically obligations of the Federal Reserve System. A part of a sound program for monetary change would involve eliminating this type of currency and replacing it with currency which represents obligations of the Treasury. Some currency of this type continues to circulate in the form of U.S. Notes, but this is a tiny fraction of existing currency. Switching the form of currency is only important as part of eliminating the money creation role of the Fed, but it also establishes a clear responsibility of the Congress for the stability of the monetary system.

In the overall program for monetary stability, the Congress would establish the rate of increase in the money supply for ten year periods. After the rate was determined, the Treasury would be instructed to print money at the appropriate rate and use that money for government fiscal operations in a normal way. Under such a system, new money would serve as a pure revenue source for government. This is not now the case and the amount involved is fairly significant. This is part of the savings in government fiscal operations referred to earlier.

Under the present system, increases in the money supply disappear into the banking system. Precisely where is not clear, but the amount involved is significant. The present size of M_1 is $270 billion (approximately). If that amount is increased at a 5 percent rate, the annual rate of increase would begin at $13½ billion and would rise from that figure through compounding. At the present time, as has been seen, the rate of increase in the money supply is greater than that and so the present figure would be greater than $13½ billion. The 5 percent figure is selected because it would be appropriate for maintaining a constant or slightly rising price level. Of the present larger figure, only the surplus profits of the Fed—an amount in the neighborhood of $3 billion—is turned over to the Treasury. Thus, the direct governmental use of new currency would result in a net increased revenue source of some $10 billions.

Monetizing Part of the National Debt

This $10 billion revenue source is also matched by a similar saving on the expenditure side of the federal budget. A move to 100 percent reserves would have to require a drastic increase in currency production. Otherwise, the money supply would fall precipitously as required reserve rates were increased. The most logical use for this replacement currency would be paying off part of the national debt—a process called "monetizing the national debt."

Currency is technically debt of the government or institution issuing it, but it is noninterest bearing debt. As such, monetizing part of the national debt would mean replacing interest-bearing debt with noninterest bearing debt. Clearly, this would result in an interest savings to the federal government.

This procedure would be accomplished by gradually increasing reserve requirements over a five-year period. During this period, potential reductions in the money supply caused by higher reserve requirements would be offset by new money that was printed by the Treasury and used to pay off national debt instruments as they come due. Under the present system, these payments would be financed by new borrowing, so the process itself would be one of not reborrowing, rather than "calling in" the debt in any sense. Done over a five year period, it would be an orderly process with no serious allocational difficulties—though one would not wish to hold bank stock during this period.

In the end, if the present money supply figure of $270 billion is employed, the debt would be reduced by $162 billion. This would be the amount necessary to offset the monetary declines that would otherwise occur with 100 percent reserves. If it is assumed that the interest rate on this amount was 6 percent, the interest savings would be $9.7 billion. This means that the total budget savings of the entire program would approach $20 billion.

Conclusion

With respect to the current Great Inflation, the United States is like a great giant floundering in a monetary mess it does not understand. It easily has the power to escape back into its previous prosperity and confidence, but it is mired in a network of unworkable solutions that only complicate its problems. Simple monetary adjustments can solve this problem, as outlined in this book. But no solution can work overnight for a problem that was nine years in the making. It will take at least four years to eradicate the inflationary expectations that exist now in our economy—four patient years of a moderately sluggish and still inflationary (though at a declining rate) economic performance. As the economy was wound up for years into inflationary expectations, it must be wound down. Attempts to turn it off will cause recessions, as has happened once already. Nor will attempts at gimmickry work. Four phases of wage and price controls have finally created Phase IV—the shortage phase. We have shortages of meat and wheat and oil, but we have no shortage of inflation. Such programs will not work except to retard economic growth and, in the process, to make monetary increases even more inflationary.

The way out is to begin reducing the rate of monetary increase slowly and systematically and to continue that policy without deviant reactions to short-term effects from now until 1977—or, if we wait a year, until 1978. There is some hope presently because the Fed's performance in the summer months of 1973 has been desirable and could be the first step in the right direction. This, however, is probably wishful thinking. At the first sign of recession, the money gates will probably be thrown open again. We need careful restraint, not dramatic policy initiatives, and it is unlikely that the Fed will provide this.

Still, the solution is easily available and it is simple. The complexity lies in inducing its implementation.

September 1973

150

How Can We Judge
What The Federal Reserve is Doing?

By Homer Jones
July 19, 1972

Within the Federal Reserve system and among outside experts, there is disagreement as to how to measure what the Federal Reserve has done and is doing. Nonetheless, the intelligent and interested layman needs to do the best he can to make a judgment as to what is happening from time to time. The following few paragraphs are written as an introductory and partial attempt at explaining some means for knowing what the Federal Reserve is doing. In reading this letter, reference should be made to the Federal Reserve Bank of St. Louis' weekly *U. S. Financial Data* and monthly *Monetary Trends*.

During recent months and years, the Federal Reserve appears to have placed increased emphasis on "the aggregates" as measures of what it is trying to do and of what it has done. "The aggregates" are a melange of magnitudes including (1) a measure of money designated as "M_1" (currency plus demand deposits), (2) a broader concept of money designated as "M_2" (M_1 plus time deposits at commercial banks other than large time C/D's), (3) reserves available to support private nonbank deposits and (4) Federal Reserve credit.

For a member of the public to try to follow what the Federal Reserve is doing, it is now necessary that he consider the course of "the aggregates." This letter proposes to give some simple indications as to how the course of the aggregates can most simply be observed and interpreted.

Sources of information for following "the aggregates" are numerous but I shall designate three which may be most useful.

(1) *Record of Policy Actions of the Federal Open Market Committee.* The F.O.M.C. generally meets every four weeks and the record is released to the public approximately 90 days following the date of the meeting. The *Record* first appears in a press release and if one wishes to be as up to date as possible, he will get on the mailing list or possibly procure the release regularly by yet more expeditious means. Otherwise, he can wait from a few days to more than a month until it appears in the subsequent *Federal Reserve Bulletin.* For example, the *Record* for the FOMC meeting of March 21, 1972 is the latest which has been made available. It appeared in a release dated June 19, which arrived in the mail June 23, and subsequently appeared in the June *Bulletin,* which arrived in the mail July 8th.

While it is desirable to have these *Records* at hand, it must be recognized that they, including the "policy directives" contained therein, are generally vague. One should not be very optimistic about learning, with reasonable accuracy, much from these *Records*—though they are the only official statement available to the public. For example, the policy directive of March 21 called for "moderate growth in monetary aggregates over the months ahead." But what is "moderate"? And since various monetary aggregates have differing trends and rates of change, especially for a period of a few months, it is quite uncertain what is intended, and it is difficult to judge whether the intentions are accomplished.

(2) *Federal Reserve Board Releases.* The second suggested

152

source is the Federal Reserve Board's statistical release, *H.9.* This appears weekly, but it wisely does not try to make anything out of changes over one or two or even three weeks. In effect, it gives the annual rate of change for each of eight "aggregates" for the past three months, the past six, and the past 12. It makes no attempt to evaluate or interpret the data.

(3) *Federal Reserve Bank of St. Louis Releases.* The third and final suggested source is the Federal Reserve Bank of St. Louis with its weekly release *U. S. Financial Data* and its monthly *Monetary Trends.* These releases, appropriately revised from time to time, have now been made to the public for about ten (10) years. That bank was presenting the "aggregates" to the public in a useful form long before the term became popular in the rest of the Federal Reserve System and in the country at large. These releases may be used together and in conjunction with the Bank's *Annual Economic Data.* In combination they permit useful analysis.

The St. Louis weekly *U. S. Financial Data* is valuable in that it brings each time series chart up to the most recent date weekly and monthly, so that current developments can be seen in some perspective. It also presents some past data and for some series contains a table of the rates of change to the present from some recent times within the past year. The St. Louis monthly *Monetary Trends* release contains rate of change data for some aggregates for which the weekly does not, and presents them somewhat further back in time. The annual data provide historical perspective for about twenty years.

Together these three periodic publications of the St. Louis Bank provide the best means available to those of us who are not specialized analysts for judging what the Federal Reserve is doing. In discussing their use as a source of current information, one could look primarily at the "monthly" and look at the "weekly" as a supplement or one can look at the "weekly" as the basic series. I shall proceed in the second manner as a point of departure in the following discussion.

The weekly release contains 11 pages of charts, data and

153

tables, and the monthly *Monetary Trends* contains 13 pages. The layman is faced with the question as to which of these aggregates he should give special attention or how he can look at all of them simultaneously and come out with any conclusion as to what the Federal Reserve has been doing from time to time.

The Federal Reserve Board Statistical Release *H.9*, entitled *Weekly Summary of Banking and Credit Statistics*, divides the "aggregates" into two categories, the "reserve aggregates" and the "monetary aggregates." The aggregates regularly presented by the Federal Reserve Bank of St. Louis are so divided in the accompanying table. The reserve aggregates are sometimes referred to as "targets" and the monetary aggregates as "indicators."

Experts will differ as to how to make use of the weekly and monthly releases, but my advice is that we laymen should concentrate on "Money Stock" (weekly, p. 5; monthly, pp. 2, 3; quarterly, p. 4; annual, p. B-2), or on "Money stock plus net time deposits" (weekly, p. 7; monthly, pp. 4, 5; annual, p. B-8). Most ideas about how "aggregates" are important in determination of total spending, final sales, real product and prices, treat "money" as the crucial magnitude.

The "Money Stock" of page 5 of the weekly is also to be found on pages 2 and 3 of the monthly and on page B-2 of the annual. (See accompanying table.) Comparable data for money on a quarterly basis are to be found on page 4 of the St. Louis Bank's *Quarterly Economic Trends*, May 31, 1972.

As an example of how these various tables may be used in conjunction with each other, we may observe that money has increased at an 8.1 percent annual rate from the 4 weeks ending January 5, when the FOMC record seems to indicate a resolve for more rapid expansion of aggregates, to the 4 weeks ending July 5, 1972 (weekly *U.S. Financial Data*, p. 5), compared with growth at only an 0.8 percent annual rate in the preceding 5 months (*Monetary Trends*, pp. 2, 3), and at a 4.1 percent rate from first quarter 1969 to fourth quarter 1970 (*Quarterly Economic Trends*, p. 4), and with a 1.9 percent rate from 1952 and 1964 (*Annual U.S. Economic Data*, p. B-2).

154

On both the weekly chart and the monthly chart, actual rates of money growth are compared with a straight line trend for the 5 year period from December, 1966 to December, 1971. The charts imply that since the rate of growth from the end of 1971 has been above the trend rate (which gave us a rapid inflation), we see no signs as yet that the FOMC is following a monetary policy that will reduce the inflation rate.

Turning to "money stock plus net time deposits" (p. 7 of weekly, p. 5 of monthly, p. B-8 of annual) we see that growth has been at an 11.3 percent rate since December (weekly data) compared with a 6.4 percent rate in the preceding 6 months and 8.9 percent in the past 12 months (monthly data) and with a 7.8 percent rate in the 1964-71 period (annual data, p. B-8).

RESERVE AND MONETARY "AGGREGATES"
(AS PRESENTED BY THE FEDERAL
RESERVE BANK OF ST. LOUIS [a])

	Weekly	Monthly	Quarterly	Annual
RESERVE AGGREGATES				
Federal Reserve Credit	p. 3	pp. 8, 9		p. A-3
Monetary Base	p. 2	pp. 8, 9		p. A-4
Total Reserves [b]				
RPD [b]	p. 3	pp. 6, 7		p. A-2
MONETARY AGGREGATES				
M_1 [b]	p. 5	pp. 2, 3	p. 4	p. B-2
Demand Deposit Component	p. 4	pp. 2, 3		p. B-3
Time Deposits [b]	p. 6	p. 5		p. B-5
Certificates of Deposit	p. 8			p. B-10
Net Times Deposits	p. 6	pp. 4, 5		p. B-11
M_2	p. 7	pp. 4, 5		p. B-8
Credit Proxy	p. 9			
Adjusted Credit Proxy [b]	p. 9			
Bank Loans & Investments		pp. 10, 11		p. C-2
Bank Loans		pp. 10, 11		p. C-3
Bank Investments		p. 11		p. C-4

[a] The pages indicated are those of the most recent presentations. Presumably the particular charts will in general appear on the same pages for considerable future time.

[b] Appears in the Federal Reserve Board's H.9 Statistical Release, "Weekly Summary of Banking and Credit Measures."

Whether M_1 (weekly, p. 5) or M_2 (p. 7) is a better indicator of monetary influence or whether they are equally good is a matter of dispute. I personally feel that on the whole M_1 is more significant and reliable, and that is where I would place primary emphasis. In any case, as the charts indicate, there is a consensus that the large certificates of deposit are not to be considered as money but simply as intermediary money market instruments.

On page 9 of the weekly are found the "credit proxy" and the "credit proxy adjusted," and on page 11 of the monthly, and on C-2 of the annual, "Bank Loans and Investments—all commercial banks." These three are similar. They put emphasis on what the Federal Reserve can do to the assets of the banks while measures of money emphasis influence on bank liabilities. I would personally not put the emphasis here and indeed it would seem that the Federal Reserve places somewhat less emphasis on bank credit measures than it did in former years.

The Board seems to find quite different adjustments necessary as between that which it makes to the credit proxy and that which it makes to time deposits. From the time deposits it subtracts the large C/D's, while to the credit proxy it adds bank related commercial paper, Eurodollar borrowings of U. S. Banks, etc.

The "reserve aggregates" are generally viewed as determining in considerable measure the money supply and other of the "monetary aggregates." In a rough way, we may say that the Federal Reserve open market operations influence the amount of Federal Reserve credit (weekly, p. 3, monthly, p. 9, annual, p. A-3); changes in Federal Reserve credit influence the amount of member bank reserves (annual, p. A-2); changes in member bank reserves influence "reserves available to support private nonbank deposits" (RPD) (weekly, p. 3, monthly, p. 7) and RPD influence the amount of bank deposits, and thereby the stock of money. The Monetary Base (weekly, p. 2, monthly, p. 9, annual, p. A-4) is a more inclusive variable, reflecting not only Federal Reserve Credit, but other variables as well, and in turn determining not only bank deposits but deposits plus the currency component of money. The multiplier (weekly, p. 2) is the observed relation between the Base and M_1.

In February, 1972, the FOMC first undertook to make use of the RPD as an intermediary objective or transmission mechanism. If this concept helps the System to achieve its objectives it is all to the good. But there is nothing at all remarkable about it. It is simply a refinement of total reserves. Changes in the money supply conform more closely to changes in RPD than to changes in total reserves (which include reserves supporting government and inter-bank deposits, which are not treated as part of the money supply). RPDs are more closely related to Federal Reserve open market operations than are total reserves and other reserve aggregates. They are less affected by decisions of the Federal Government and of the commercial banks. The Federal Reserve Bank of St. Louis, long ago, with an eye to the demand deposit component of M_1, used the concept of "reserves available for private demand deposits."

A distinguishing characteristic of the weekly *U. S. Financial Data* and the monthly *Monetary Trends* is their "triangular" tables. These tables are designed for two purposes:

1. They permit the user to read off the annual rate of change of the magnitude concerned from any point in the time period to any other point. "Annual rate of change" provides a common denominator for comparing the rate of growth or decline in one sub-period with that in any other sub-period. There is no absolute virtue in using the "annual" rate but it is conventional. As an example of this use we may refer to the monthly *Monetary Trends* released July 19, 1972. The table on money stock (i.e. M_1) at the top of page 2. For convenience of exposition, a copy of this particular table is included herewith. Here we can read, by observing the figure in the lower right-hand corner, that the rate of change from May to June was 4.7 percent per annum, and, by observing the figure in the lower left hand corner, that the rate from November, 1970 to June, 1971 was 6.7 percent per annum. To give one more example, one can observe that the rate of increase from July, 1971 to January, 1972 was 1.2 percent per annum (the figure just below the figure "0.8" which appears in a box).

157

Reproduced from "Monetary Trends" Dated July 19, 1972

MONEY STOCK

COMPOUNDED ANNUAL RATES OF CHANGE

Terminal Month	11-70	12-70	1-71	2-71	3-71	4-71	5-71	6-71	7-71	8-71	9-71	10-71	11-71	12-71	1-72	2-72	3-72	4-72	5-72	Billions of Dollars
																				Initial Month
12-70	7.0																			214.8
1-71	4.9	2.8																		215.3
2-71	7.9	8.4	14.2																	217.7
3-71	8.8	9.4	12.9	11.6																219.7
4-71	8.8	9.2	11.4	10.0	8.5															221.2
5-71	9.8	10.4	12.3	11.7	11.7	15.1														223.8
6-71	9.7	10.2	11.7	11.1	11.0	12.2	9.5													225.5
7-71	9.8	10.3	11.6	11.0	10.9	11.7	10.0	10.6												227.4
8-71	9.1	9.4	10.3	9.7	9.3	9.5	7.7	6.8	3.2											228.0
9-71	7.9	8.0	8.7	7.9	7.3	7.1	5.2	3.8	0.5	-2.1										227.6
10-71	7.2	7.2	7.8	7.0	6.3	6.0	4.2	3.0	0.5	-0.8	0.5									227.7
11-71	6.6	6.6	7.0	6.2	5.5	5.1	3.5	2.4	0.4	-0.5	0.3	0.0								227.7
12-71	6.3	6.2	6.6	5.8	5.2	4.8	3.4	2.4	0.8	0.3	1.1	1.3	2.7							228.2
1-72	6.1	6.0	6.3	5.6	5.0	4.6	3.4	2.5	1.2	0.8	1.6	1.9	2.9	3.2						228.8
2-72	6.5	6.5	6.8	6.2	5.7	5.4	4.4	3.8	2.9	2.8	3.8	4.7	6.3	8.2	13.3					231.2
3-72	6.9	6.9	7.2	6.7	6.3	6.1	5.2	4.8	4.1	4.2	5.3	6.2	7.8	9.6	13.0	12.6				233.5
4-72	7.0	7.0	7.3	6.8	6.4	6.2	5.5	5.1	4.5	4.6	5.6	6.5	7.9	9.2	11.3	10.3	8.0			235.0
5-72	6.8	6.8	7.0	6.6	6.2	6.0	5.3	4.9	4.4	4.5	5.4	6.1	7.2	8.1	9.3	8.0	5.8	3.6		235.7
6-72	6.7	6.7	6.9	6.4	6.1	5.9	5.3	4.9	4.4	4.5	5.3	5.9	6.8	7.5	8.4	7.2	5.4	4.2	4.7	236.6
	11-70	12-70	1-71	2-71	3-71	4-71	5-71	6-71	7-71	8-71	9-71	10-71	11-71	12-71	1-72	2-72	3-72	4-72	5-72	

Annotations on chart: +11.6%, +0.8%, +7.5%

Prepared by Federal Reserve Bank of St. Louis
July 14, 1972

DEMAND DEPOSIT COMPONENT OF MONEY
COMPOUNDED ANNUAL RATES OF CHANGE

Terminal Month	Initial Month																			Billions of Dollars
	11-70	12-70	1-71	2-71	3-71	4-71	5-71	6-71	7-71	8-71	9-71	10-71	11-71	12-71	1-72	2-72	3-72	4-72	5-72	
12-70	6.8																			165.8
1-71	4.1	1.5																		166.0
2-71	7.7	8.2	15.5																	168.0
3-71	9.0	9.7	14.1	12.8																169.7
4-71	8.7	9.1	11.8	10.0	7.3															170.7
5-71	10.1	10.7	13.2	12.4	12.2	17.4														173.0
6-71	10.2	10.8	12.7	12.1	11.8	14.1	10.9													174.5
7-71	10.1	10.6	12.2	11.5	11.2	12.5	10.1	9.3												175.8
8-71	9.3	9.6	10.9	10.1	9.6	10.2	7.9	6.4	3.5											176.3
9-71	7.9	8.0	8.9	8.0	7.2	7.2	4.8	2.8	-0.3	-4.0										175.7
10-71	7.0	7.1	7.7	6.8	5.9	5.7	3.5	1.7	-0.7	-2.7	-1.4									175.5
11-71	6.4	6.4	6.9	6.0	5.2	4.9	2.9	1.4	-0.5	-1.8	-0.7	0.0								175.5
12-71	6.0	6.0	6.4	5.5	4.7	4.4	2.7	1.4	-0.1	-1.0	0.0	0.7	1.4							175.7
1-72	5.7	5.7	6.0	5.2	4.5	4.2	2.6	1.5	0.2	-0.4	0.5	1.1	1.7	2.1						176.0
2-72	6.3	6.3	6.7	6.0	5.3	5.2	3.9	3.0	2.2	1.9	3.2	4.3	5.8	8.1	14.5					178.0
3-72	6.7	6.7	7.1	6.5	6.0	5.9	4.8	4.1	3.5	3.5	4.8	6.1	7.7	9.9	14.1	13.6				179.9
4-72	6.8	6.8	7.1	6.5	6.1	6.0	5.0	4.4	3.0	3.9	5.1	6.2	7.5	9.1	11.6	10.2	6.9			180.9
5-72	6.6	6.6	6.9	6.3	5.9	5.8	4.9	4.3	3.8	3.9	4.9	5.8	6.8	8.0	9.5	7.9	5.1	3.4		181.4
6-72	6.4	6.4	6.7	6.2	5.8	5.6	4.8	4.3	3.9	3.9	4.8	5.6	6.4	7.3	8.4	6.9	4.8	3.7	4.0	182.0
	11-70	12-70	1-71	2-71	3-71	4-71	5-71	6-71	7-71	8-71	9-71	10-71	11-71	12-71	1-72	2-72	3-72	4-72	5-72	

+12.2%

−0.1%

+7.3%

Prepared by Federal Reserve Bank of St. Louis
July 14, 1972

159

2. The second use of this type of table is to quickly make a judgment distinguishing periods of high and periods of low rates of increase, that is, periods of relatively rapid and periods of relatively slow monetary expansion. Referring to the same table on page 2 of *Monetary Trends,* we see that from January to July, 1971 the annual rate was 11.6 percent. This period was presumably especially designated upon a basis of observing that the rates month by month during this period were relatively high. But there is nothing sacrosanct about the terminal points of the period. Any user of the table may read off the rate of change for any other period that he considers significant. It is simply a first approximation to say that the three brackets and figures here emphasized indicate stimulative monetary expansion January-July, 1971 (11.6 percent), relatively restrictive action from July to December (0.8 percent), and again relatively rapid expansion since December (7.5 percent).

The triangular tables proliferated by the Federal Reserve Bank of St. Louis in its many other releases are to be interpreted similarly. For example, in its monthly *National Economic Trends* one may read off at a glance from any selected month to any other selected month the rate of increase of employment, industrial production, retail sales, personal income, consumer prices, etc. In that and other releases, we may also find a basis for selecting periods of relatively rapid and relatively slow increase.

In considering these rate of change tables, it may be worthwhile to mention a peculiarity of those contained in the weekly *U. S. Financial Data.* Let us look at the table for "Money Stock" on page 5. Here we can read that from the average of four weeks ending January 5th to the average of four weeks ending July 5th, the money stock (M_1) increased at an 8.1 percent annual rate. The reason for using an average of four weeks is that weekly movements are quite erratic and comparing one particular week with some other particular week might give quite misleading and rapidly fluctuating results. At the same time, it makes possible using the weekly information and keeping up to date.